A Talk Given on
A COURSE IN MIRACLES

A Talk Given on
A COURSE IN MIRACLES®

An Introduction

Seventh Edition

KENNETH WAPNICK, Ph.D.

Foundation for A COURSE IN MIRACLES®

Foundation for A Course in Miracles®
41397 Buecking Drive
Temecula, CA 92590
www.facim.org

Printed in the United States of America

First edition, 1983, Second printing, 1985,
Second edition, revised and enlarged, 1987,
Third edition, revised and enlarged, 1989,
Fifth printing, 1991, Fourth edition, 1992,
Fifth edition, 1993, Sixth edition, 1996,
Seventh edition, 1999, Tenth printing, 2006

Portions of *A Course in Miracles* copyright 1975, 1992
by the *Foundation for A Course in Miracles*®

Library of Congress Cataloging-in-Publication Data

Wapnick, Kenneth
    A talk given on a Course in miracles : an introduction / Kenneth Wapnick. -- 4th ed.
    p.   cm.
    ISBN 13: 978-0-933291-16-4
    ISBN 10: 0-933291-16-7
    1. Course in miracles. 2. Spiritual life. I. Title.
BP605.C68W36 1992
299'.93--dc20
                                            92-30373

CONTENTS

Preface to the Seventh Edition

This current edition has been revised to include references for scriptural passages. Readers may note that some passages, although enclosed in quotation marks, are not verbatim renderings of the verses cited in the references. We have kept the wording of the original informal oral presentation. Aside from this and other minor editorial revisions, the book is the same as the previous edition.

Preface to Sixth Edition

In this new edition, the notation for references to *A Course in Miracles* are for the second edition only. Aside from this revision, as well as another typesetting, the book remains unchanged from the previous edition.

Preface to Fifth Edition

For this new edition, the book has been retypeset once again. An index of references to *A Course in Miracles* has been included as well. Aside from this addition, the book remains virtually unchanged from the previous edition.

Preface to Fourth Edition

For this new edition, the book has again been retypeset. However, virtually no changes have been made from the third edition, except in the notation for references to *A Course in Miracles*. This was necessitated by the recently published (1992) second edition of the Course, which was retypeset and contains numbering for all paragraphs and sentences, as well as for the chapters and sections of the text, lessons and introductions in the workbook for students, questions in the manual for teachers, and the terms in the clarification of terms. Thus, references to *A Course in Miracles* are now given in two ways: the first, unchanged from before, cites the pages found in the first edition; the second is now consistent with the numbering system of the second edition. An example from each book follows:

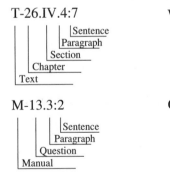

T-26.IV.4:7

| Sentence
| Paragraph
| Section
| Chapter
| Text

W-pI.169.5:2

| Sentence
| Paragraph
| Lesson
| Part I
| Workbook

M-13.3:2

| Sentence
| Paragraph
| Question
| Manual

C-6.4:6

| Sentence
| Paragraph
| Term
| Clarification of Terms

Preface to Third Edition

This third edition requires an explanation. The popularity of the original pamphlet has indeed been surprising and, in preparing for its fourth printing we felt it deserved a face lift: thus, this new format of the "Talk" in book form, and the added subtitle to better identify its subject matter. As in the other editions, the basic material has been left unchanged. However, improvements have been made: specific references for quotations from *A Course in Miracles* have been supplied, some material in the later chapters has been rearranged, chapter titles have been changed to conform better to the actual content of the chapters, and charts from other publications have been interspersed in the text for clarification of some of the principles. Finally, a more appropriate ending has been added. For some reason, the actual conclusion of the original one-day workshop was never recorded, and the transcription of the talk, as well as the published pamphlet, ended abruptly. It thus seemed time to give the presentation a proper conclusion. While I could never recall my words of almost nine years ago, I have provided what seems to be a suitable closing statement.

For this new edition, we have also included information about our Foundation, and the Conference and Retreat Center that has begun since the last printing. It is our hope at the Foundation for *A Course in Miracles* that this revised edition will better serve the needs of students of the Course for a simple though comprehensive introduction to the basic principles of this important spiritual document.

As always, I am very grateful to my wife, Gloria, the Vice-President of the Foundation, for her ongoing fidelity and commitment to maintaining the integrity of *A Course in Miracles* in general, and to the Foundation's publications in particular, not to mention her specific suggestions for this new format of the "Talk." I am also very grateful to Rosemarie LoSasso, the Foundation's Publications Director, for her faithful dedication to the carrying out of our Foundation's vision, in form and content, and for her specific help in the preparation of this revised edition.

Preface to Second Edition

As the pamphlet was entering its third printing with translations into Spanish and Dutch being prepared, I thought I should give it another look. I had not really read the pamphlet since its original publication and I began to read it with some apprehensions. It was about four years since the first publication, and about six since the original workshop, and I knew that there would be many things I would state differently. However, I was pleasantly surprised as to how well the pamphlet held up. To be sure, there were statements I would have liked to make that I had not; some points I would have stated differently; yet overall I felt that the presentation nicely emphasized some of the more essential points of the Course.

Interestingly enough, the Dutch translator, Gerben Andriessen, sent me a tape of the original workshop, from which the initial transcript was taken. This was the first time I had heard the tape, and discovered that approximately one-fifth of the Connecticut talk had been omitted in the transcription. While nothing was missing that substantively detracted from the talk, the omission nonetheless consisted of relevant material that enhanced the presentation. I have therefore restored almost all of this material, making for a larger and richer publication. In addition, I have made some minor changes to the original published material, including additional sentences to clarify the presentation in a few places, and some general "cleaning up" of sloppy grammar, sentence structure, etc.

Despite these changes, the informal quality of the "Talk" has been preserved, keeping to its being a transcription of an actual talk, and not a more formal written presentation. I thus am pleased that I was able to resist the temptation to rewrite the pamphlet, which basically stands as it did originally, and now, even more so, is faithful to the original talk.

I am very grateful to my wife, Gloria, for her careful reading of the various phases of the pamphlet's life and, as always, for her helpful comments and suggestions, and to Rosemarie LoSasso for graciously reading the manuscript with a critical eye and supervising the printing of this revised edition.

Preface to First Edition

This is a transcript of a one-day workshop I gave in Madison, Connecticut, May 9, 1981, as part of a nine-day retreat conducted by Tara Singh. We are publishing it now in response to many requests for a succinct presentation of the principles of *A Course in Miracles* and specifically for the transcript of this workshop. Hopefully, this pamphlet will meet this need. It is printed virtually as the workshop was given, with only very minor changes to improve its readability. However, for an in-depth presentation of the Course's principles, along with their implications for our everyday living and the Course's relationship to Christianity, the reader is invited to consult my *Forgiveness and Jesus: The Meeting Place of A COURSE IN MIRACLES and Christianity* (published by the Foundation for *A Course in Miracles*, 41397 Buecking Drive, Temecula, CA 92590).

I am grateful to Emily LeVier of Mahwah, NJ, for supplying me with this transcript a year ago and first suggesting its printing, and I am especially grateful to the anonymous person on the retreat who typed from the tape of the workshop.

Addendum to Second Printing

The "anonymous person" is Fred Marsh of Los Alamos, New Mexico.

Chapter 1

THE STORY OF *A COURSE IN MIRACLES*

One of the interesting things about how *A Course in Miracles* came to be written is that the very process of its being taken down, and the story around it, provide a perfect example of just what the basic principles of the Course itself are. The central message of the Course is that salvation comes at any instant that two people join together to share a common interest or work for a common goal. This will always involve some aspect of forgiveness, which we will talk about later.

The two people responsible for *A Course in Miracles* were Helen Schucman, who died in February 1981, and William Thetford.* They were psychologists at the Columbia Presbyterian Medical Center in New York City. Bill had gotten there first, in 1958, and was the Director of the Psychology Department. Helen joined him a few months after that. For the first seven years of their relationship they had a great deal of difficulty with each other. Their personalities were entirely opposite. While they worked well together on

_____

* William Thetford died in July 1988.

1

one level, on a personal level there was a lot of tension and ambivalence. Not only was there difficulty because of their own relationship, but they had difficulty with other members of the Department, other departments within the Medical Center, and in working with other disciplines in other medical centers. It was typical of the atmosphere in a large university or medical center, and Columbia was no different from any other.

The turning point came one spring day in 1965 when Helen and Bill had to go crosstown to the Cornell Medical Center, where they had a regular interdisciplinary meeting. These were usually ugly affairs, with a lot of competitiveness and backbiting; the kind of thing that is again very common in a university setting. Helen and Bill were very much a part of that as well, being critical and judgmental of other people. But this one day, just prior to their leaving for the meeting, Bill, who was a rather quiet and unassuming man, did something very out of character for him. He made an impassioned speech to Helen in which he said he thought there had to be a better way of dealing with these meetings and the kind of problems that were arising. He felt that they should be more loving and accepting, rather than so filled with competition and criticism.

Equally unexpected and out of character was Helen's response: She agreed with him and pledged to help him find this other way. Their agreement was very out of keeping for both of them, as they tended to be critical rather than accepting of each other. Their joining with each other was an example of what the Course refers to as a holy instant and, as I said at the beginning, the holy instant is the means of salvation.

On a level at which neither of them was aware, that instant acted as the signal that opened up the door to a whole series of experiences that Helen began to have, both waking as well as in her dreams. I will mention a few of them which have a strong psychic nature as well as a strong religious aspect, for the figure of Jesus began to appear more and more regularly. What made this a little unexpected was the position that Helen had taken at that point in her life. She was in her fifties and had adopted the role of a very militant atheist, cleverly disguising her bitter resentment against a God she felt had not done well by her. Thus she was aggressive towards any kind of thinking that she judged as fuzzy or ambiguous and not capable of being studied, measured, or evaluated. She was a very good research psychologist, and had a keen, analytical, and logical mind with no tolerance for any kind of thinking that deviated from that.

Helen had, from the time she was a little girl, a kind of psychic ability such as seeing things that were not there. However, she never really paid too much attention to it, thinking that everyone did that. She had one or two rather striking mystical experiences at an early age, to which she also paid no attention. In fact, she had hardly mentioned it to anyone up to now. It was thus very surprising that she began to have all of these experiences. The experiences also frightened her a great deal; part of her was afraid that she was going crazy. These were not normal things, and if Bill had not been there to support and encourage her, I think that she would have stopped the whole process.

It is very important to recognize how essential Bill's help and constant joining with Helen was. Otherwise, *A Course in Miracles* would never have been recorded. Thus you are now seeing another example of the basic principle of the Course itself, expressed over and over again in many different ways: "Salvation is a collaborative venture" (T-4.VI.8:2), "The ark of peace is entered two by two" (T-20.IV.6:5), "No one can enter Heaven by himself" (W-pI.134.17:7), and "together, or not at all" (T-19.IV-D.12:8). If it were not for the joining of Helen and Bill in this enterprise, there would not be a Course, and we would not be gathered here today to speak about it.

One whole series of experiences that Helen had came during the summer, almost like a serial. It came to her in different waking segments; it was not a dream state. The series began with her walking along a deserted beach and finding a boat on the sand. She realized that it was her job to get the boat off the beach and into the water. There was no way that she could have done that, however, as it was too stuck in the sand. In the middle of this, a stranger appeared and he offered to help her. In the bottom of the boat Helen then noticed what she described as an ancient sending and receiving set. She said to the stranger, "Maybe this will help us." But he said, "You are not ready for that yet. Just leave it alone." But he got the boat off the beach and into the water. Whenever there would be trouble and stormy seas, this man would always appear to help her. After a while she recognized that the man was Jesus, although he did not resemble the usual image people have of him. He was always around to help her when the going got tough.

Finally, in the last scene of this series, the boat reached its destination in what seemed to be a canal, where everything was calm and still and peaceful. There was a fishing rod in the bottom of the boat, and at the end of the line at the bottom of the sea was a treasure chest. Helen saw the treasure chest and became all excited, for at that time in her life she was very fond of jewelry and all kinds of pretty things. She was looking forward to finding what would be in the chest. She lifted up the chest but was very disappointed when she opened it up and saw this big black book. That was all there was in the chest. On the spine of the book was written the name Aesculapius, the Greek god of healing. At that point, Helen did not

5

recognize the name. It was not until many years later, when the Course was finally all typed out and placed in black thesis binders, that she and Bill realized that it looked exactly like the book that she had found in the treasure chest. She saw the same treasure chest again, and this time it had a string of pearls around it. A few days later, she had a dream in which a stork was flying over some villages, and in its pouch was a black book with a gold cross on it. And a voice said to her, "This is your book." (This was prior to the time when the Course actually came.)

There was another very interesting experience that Helen had in which she saw herself walking into a cave. It was a very ancient cave and on its floor was what looked like a Torah scroll with two rods, around which the parchment is wound. (The Torah is the first part of the Old Testament.) It was very ancient. In fact, the little string that tied it together fell off and disintegrated as Helen picked it up. She looked at the scroll and unrolled it, and on the center panel were the words, "GOD IS." She thought that was very nice. Then she unrolled it a little bit more and there was a blank panel on the left and a blank panel on the right. And this voice said to her, "If you look at the left you will be able to read everything that ever happened in the past. And if you look to the right you will be able to read everything that will ever happen in the future."

But she said, "No I am not interested in that. All I want is the center panel."

So Helen rolled the scroll back so that the only thing she saw were the words, "GOD IS." Then the voice said to her, "Thank you. This time you made it." She recognized at that time that she had passed some kind of test that evidently she had not been able to do before. What this really meant was that she had expressed a desire not to misuse the ability that she had; in other words, not to use it for any kind of power or curiosity. The only thing that she was really looking for was the present, where God is found.

One workbook lesson says, "We say 'God is' and then we cease to speak," because there is nothing more to say beyond those two words (W-pI.169.5:4). I think that passage refers back to this experience of the cave. There is a strong emphasis throughout the Course on the ideas that the past no longer exists and that we should not be concerned about the future, which also does not exist. We should only be concerned with the present, since that is the only place we can know God.

One final story: Helen and Bill were going to the Mayo Clinic in Rochester, Minnesota, to spend a day studying how the psychologists there did their psychological evaluations. The preceding night, Helen saw a very clear picture in her mind of a church which she first thought was Catholic but then realized was Lutheran. She saw it so clearly that she sketched it. As she was looking down on it in her vision, she became convinced that she and Bill would see this church as their plane was landing in Rochester. This church, then, became a very powerful symbol of whether or not she was sane, as by this time she was doubting her own sanity and could not really understand all these inner experiences. She felt if she could see this church it would reassure her that she was not crazy. When they landed, however, they did not see the church. Helen became frantic, and so Bill hired a cab to take them to every church in Rochester. I think there were about twenty-six churches in town, but they did not find Helen's church. Helen was quite upset, but there was nothing more to do that night.

The next day was a busy one and that evening they headed back to New York. While waiting at the airport, Bill, who had always been very good at this kind of thing, happened to pick up a book on Rochester he thought Helen's husband Louis might like to see. It included a history of the Mayo Clinic and, as Bill was leafing through, he saw a picture of the exact church Helen had described. It was on the old site of the Mayo Clinic, for the church had been razed in order to build the Clinic. Helen looked down on it because it was no longer there; she was looking down on it in time. That made her feel somewhat better, but that was not the end of the story.

Helen and Bill had to change planes in Chicago. It was already late at night and they were very tired. They were sitting in the terminal, and Helen saw a woman sitting across the waiting area, minding her own business. Helen picked up that the woman was very upset, even though there were no external signs to that effect. She went over to the woman, something she would not typically do, but she really felt compelled to do so. Sure enough, the woman was very upset. She had just run away from her husband and children and was going to New York, which she had never been to before. She had only three hundred dollars that she was going to use to stay in New York and, finally, was terrified as she had also never flown before. Helen befriended her and brought her over to Bill and, together, they took care of her on the plane. She sat between them, and told Helen at one point that she planned to stay at the Lutheran church, since she was Lutheran. Helen then heard an inner voice: "And this is my real church." Helen understood Jesus to mean that a real church is not a building, but helping and joining with another person.

When they arrived in New York, Helen and Bill put their new friend in a hotel and, curiously enough, they kept running into her during the next few days. I think

Bill once met her at Bloomingdale's, a large department store in New York, and Helen had her over for dinner once or twice. The woman eventually went back to her family, but continued to keep in touch with Helen, sending her Christmas cards, etc. One time she called Helen when I was there. This story is important for demonstrating that it is not the psychic phenomenon in itself that is important, but rather the spiritual purpose underlying it; in this case, that of helping another person.

One day in mid-October, Helen said to Bill, "I think I will do something very unexpected." At that point Bill suggested she get a notebook and write down all the things that she would think or hear, or any dreams that she had. Helen began to do this. She knew shorthand and was able to write down very quickly. One evening a couple of weeks after that, she heard this voice say to her, "This is a course in miracles. Please take notes." She was so panic-stricken that she called Bill on the phone and said, "This voice keeps saying these words to me. What should I do?" Bill said something for which future generations will call him very blessed indeed. He said, "Why don't you do what the voice says?" Helen did. She began to take down the dictation and seven years later it ended up as the three books that we now have, called *A Course in Miracles*.

Helen's experience with the voice was like an internal tape recorder. She could turn the voice on and off as she wished. However, she could not "turn it off" for too long or she became upset. She was able to write down what the voice said although the voice spoke very quickly. So Helen's shorthand came in very handy. And she did this while she was fully conscious. This was not automatic writing; she was not in a trance or anything else. She could be writing and the telephone would ring; she would put down her pen, take care of the business on the phone, and then go back and finish up wherever she was. Often she would be able to pick it up in the same place. This becomes all the more remarkable when you realize that much of the Course is written in blank verse, iambic pentameter, and she would do this sort of thing and not lose the meter or the sense of what the voice was saying.

Perhaps the most frightening thing of all for Helen in this experience was that the voice identified himself as Jesus. A good part of the Course is written in the first person, where Jesus speaks a great deal about his own crucifixion. There is no mistaking the identity of the voice. The Course says, however, that it is not necessary to believe that it is the voice of Jesus to benefit from what *A Course in Miracles* says. I think it makes it easier if you do, so that you do not have to do mental gymnastics as you are reading it. But it is not

11

necessary in order to practice the principles of the Course. The Course itself says that. There is a section on Jesus in the teacher's manual which says that it is not necessary to accept Jesus into our lives, but that he would help us all the more if we let him (C-5.6:6-7).

There was no question in Helen's mind that the voice was that of Jesus, and this just made it all the more fearful for her. It was not a happy experience for her. She did it because she believed that somehow this was what she was supposed to do. At one point, she complained rather bitterly to Jesus: "Why did you choose me? Why didn't you choose a nice holy nun, or someone like that? I am the last person in the world who should be doing this." And he said, "I don't know why you say that because after all, you are doing it." She could not argue with him as she was already doing it, and obviously she was a perfect choice for it.

She would write down the words of the Course every day, usually in her steno notebook. The next day, whenever time would allow in their busy schedule, she would dictate to Bill what had been dictated to her, and he would then type it out. Bill has jokingly said that he usually had to have one arm around Helen to hold her up, while typing with the other. Helen had a great deal of difficulty even reading what she had written down. That is how *A Course in Miracles* originally came to be taken down. Again, the process occurred over a seven-year period.

The Course consists of three books, as most of you know: a text, a workbook for students, and a manual for teachers. The text, which is the most difficult of the three books to read, contains the basic theory of the Course. The workbook consists of 365 lessons, one for each day of the year, and is important as the practical application of the principles of the text. The teacher's manual is a much shorter book, and is the easiest of the three books to read as it consists of answers to some of the more likely questions a person might have. It actually is a good summary of many of the principles of the Course. Almost as an appendix is a section on the clarification of terms, which was done a number of years after *A Course in Miracles* itself was finished. This was an attempt to define some of the words that are used. If you do not already know what the words mean, however, reading that section will not help; but it contains some very lovely passages.

Helen and Bill made no corrections. The books as you have them now are essentially the way they were transmitted. The only changes that were made came about because the text came straight through and was not broken up into sections and chapters. Neither punctuation nor paragraphing was given. Helen and Bill did the initial work of structuring the text, and when I came along in 1973 I went through the entire manuscript with Helen. All of the sectioning and titling was therefore done by us. The workbook was not a problem because it came with the lessons, and the teacher's manual came with the questions and answers. It was basically in the text that this problem existed, but very often the original material was dictated in logical sections so that the breaking off into sections and chapters was not difficult. Throughout it all, we felt that we were acting according to Jesus' guidance so that everything we did would be as he wanted it.

When the Course first began, there was a lot of personal material that was given to Helen and Bill to help them understand what was happening, and how to help each other. This included a lot of material to help them accept what was being given. Since Helen and Bill were psychologists, there was material given on Freud and other people to help them bridge the gap between what they knew and what the Course was saying. Jesus instructed Helen and Bill to take out this material for obvious reasons, as it was not germane to the basic teaching of the Course. The only problem that this raised is that it left some gaps, just because of style. So sometimes we would add a phrase or two, not because of content, but just to help smooth over a transition. This occurred only right at the beginning.

The style of the first four chapters was always a problem for us. They are some of the most difficult parts to read. I think this is because of the personal material that was taken out, which made reading a little choppy. We tried to do the best we could to smooth it out. Also, at the beginning, Helen was so terrified of what was happening that while her hearing was not impaired in terms of the meaning of what was said, the style and phrasing frequently were.

Right at the beginning, for example, the words "Holy Spirit" were not usually used. Helen was so afraid of that term that Jesus used a phrase called the Spiritual Eye. This was later replaced with "the Holy Spirit," as instructed by Jesus. The word "Christ" was not usually used at the beginning either, for the same reason, but was dictated later on. But after the first month or two, Helen became more settled, and from Chapter 5 on, the Course is virtually the way that it was given.

The other thing that was not put in was capitalization. Helen's tendency to capitalize any word even remotely associated with God became the bane of my existence: which words would be capitalized and which would not. There were some words, however, that Jesus did insist were to be capitalized to help with the understanding.

Helen, who was a compulsive and a very fine editor when she was editing things for research publications, was very tempted to change certain words to fit her own stylistic preferences. But she was always told not to do that, and she did not. This required a great deal

15

of will power. There were some times when she changed words; however, she had an uncanny memory and could recall when she did that. She would find two or three hundred pages later that the reason that a specific word had been chosen was that it would be referred to later on. So she always went back and changed the word that she had changed herself.

A Course in Miracles was finished in the fall of 1972, and I met Helen and Bill in the winter of that same year. A mutual friend of ours, who was a priest-psychologist and did some of his training under Helen and Bill, knew about the Course. He and I had become friendly that fall. At that point I was on my way to Israel, and just before I left he insisted that I meet these two friends of his. We spent an evening together and some mention was made of this book on spirituality that Helen had written. Nothing more was said, however, about what it was or where it came from.

We met in Bill's apartment and I remember his pointing in the corner to where there was a stack of seven big thesis binders that contained the Course. At that point, I was taking practically nothing with me to Israel, and I really did not think that I should start with this tome. But I was very intrigued with whatever they said, although they had said very little. Later that evening I accompanied the priest to his residence where he said that he had a copy of this book if I would like to see it. I felt very strongly that I should not do so then, but all the time I was in Israel I kept thinking of this book. I had written Helen a letter and said that I was interested in seeing her book when I got back. She later told me that I had spelled "Book" with a capital "B"; I was not aware of doing that. Capitalizing words is not something that I usually do, but evidently I did it then.

As I said, all the time I was in Israel I kept thinking of this book, and I thought that there was something important in it for me. I came back in the spring of 1973, intending at that point just to spend some time visiting my family and friends, and then to go back to Israel to stay in a monastery for an indefinite period. But I was very interested in seeing this book and I made a point of going to see Helen and Bill. From the moment I saw it, I changed my plans to go back to Israel, and decided to stay in New York City.

From my point of view, *A Course in Miracles* is the best integration I have ever seen of psychology and spirituality. At that point, I did not really know there was something missing in my spiritual life, but when I saw the Course I realized that that was indeed what I had been looking for. So once you find what you are looking for, you stay with it.

One of the things which is important to know about the Course is that it makes it very clear that it is not the only way to Heaven. It says at the beginning of the teacher's manual that it is just one form of the universal course, among thousands of others (M-1.4:1-2). *A Course in Miracles* is not for all people, and it would be a mistake to think that it is. Nothing is for all people. I think that it *is* a rather important way that has been introduced into this world, but it is not for everyone. To those for whom it is not the way, the Holy Spirit will give something else.

It would be a mistake for a person to struggle with the Course when he or she does not really feel comfortable with it, and then feel that he or she has been a failure. That would really go against everything the Course itself would say. It is not its purpose to make people guilty! It is just the opposite. But for those people for whom it is the way, it is worth the struggle through it.

Q: I had understood at one time that there have been many people who start it, but that there is a tremendous resistance.

A: Absolutely right! In fact, if anyone has gone through the Course without going through some period when they throw it out the window, down the toilet, or at someone, then they are probably not doing the Course. The reasons for this we will talk about later in more detail, but the general reason is that *A Course in Miracles* goes against everything that we believe. And there is nothing that we hold to more

18

tenaciously than our belief system, right or wrong. There is a line in the Course that asks, "Do you prefer that you be right or happy?" (T-29.VII.1:9). Most of us would prefer to be right, not happy. So the Course really goes against this, and is painstaking in its description of how wrong the ego is. Since we are all very much identified with that ego, we will fight against this system. And again, I really do mean that there is something wrong if at some point or another a student does not experience resistance or difficulty with it.

At the time when the Course was first being taken down, there was literally a handful of people who knew about it, and maybe not even a full hand. Helen and Bill both treated it as if it were a deep, dark, guilty secret. Hardly anyone among their families, friends, or colleagues knew anything about it. As part of the "plan," just before the Course came into being, they were given a set of offices that were very secluded and private. They were able to get all of this material done without interfering with their work, in spite of the fact that during that period they were extremely busy. However, no one knew what they were doing. They literally kept it in the closet as a very well-kept secret, and this was still the case when I came along.

The first year I was with Helen and Bill was spent in going through the whole manuscript until everything was the way it was supposed to be. All the titles were checked, and Helen and I went through it word by word. This process took about a year and when the manuscript was finished we had it retyped. So somewhere near the end of 1974 or the early part of 1975 the whole Course was ready. But we did not know what it was ready for. It was still in the closet, so to speak, but we knew that it was ready.

In the spring of 1975 the next person showed up, and this was Judith Skutch. How she came along is an interesting story that I will not go into now, but unexpected things led to unexpected things and she appeared with Douglas Dean. Some of you may know Douglas, who is a famous parapsychologist. They came up to the Medical Center one afternoon, seemingly for some other purpose. We felt that we should share the Course with Judy and Douglas, which we did. At that point it was almost as if it left our hands and went into hers for the next step. This eventually led to the Course being published. This was not anything in which we had any expertise, and we did not feel that it was our responsibility. We thought that it was our responsibility, however, to see that it got into the hands of the right person and that it had to be done in the right way, but that we would not be agents of that. This was Judy's role and she did it very well indeed.

You will notice in the books that the copyright date is 1975, although the books were not printed until 1976. That summer a friend of Judy's in California made a photo-offset of the Course, and there were 300 copies printed that way. *A Course in Miracles* itself was not printed in the form in which you have it until 1976. And that involved one "miracle" after another. It truly was "miraculous" how quickly it all occurred. The books were first out in June of 1975, and now (2006) there have been over fifty printings.

The Foundation for Inner Peace publishes and disseminates *A Course in Miracles*. The Course is not a movement or religion; it is not another church. It is rather a system whereby individuals may find their own path to God and practice its principles. As most of you know, there are groups all over the country that spring up on their own, and we always felt it was very important that there not be any organization that functioned as an authoritative body.

None of us wanted to be placed in the role of guru. Helen was always clear on that. People would come and almost literally sit at her feet, and she would almost step on their heads. She really did not want any part of being made into the central figure of the Course. She felt the central figure of *A Course in Miracles* was Jesus or the Holy Spirit, and that was how it should be. That was very important to her. To do anything else was to set up a church-type structure, which would be the last thing in the world the author of the Course would want.

Q: How were various people able to support themselves over the course of these years?

A: Helen and Bill both had full-time jobs and I had a part-time position at the Medical Center, as well as a part-time practice of psychotherapy. I was able to fulfill my responsibilities quickly, so that the rest of the time Helen and I spent editing the Course and doing what had to be done. It was all done in our "spare time," but I think our jobs at that point were our spare time. However, while the Course was coming through, Helen and Bill were extremely busy with their various duties.

Q: Was anything ever said about the timing of it? Why it came at this time?

A: Yes. At the beginning of the dictation Helen was given an explanation for what was happening. She was told that there was a "celestial speed-up."* The world was in pretty bad shape, Jesus told her, which is obvious to anybody who looks around. This was in the mid-1960s, and the world seems to be in even

---

* For a more accurate description of "celestial speed-up," please see my *Absence from Felicity*, pp. 287-88, 464-65.

worse shape now. People were in a great deal of trouble and some were being asked to contribute their particular abilities toward this celestial speed-up, as an aid in setting things right in the world. Helen and Bill were only two of many who were contributing their particular abilities toward this plan. In the last fifteen years or so there has been a proliferation of material that is claimed to be inspired. The purpose of all this is to aid in changing people's minds about the nature of the world. Again, *A Course in Miracles* is only one of many ways. That is important. I emphasize this because of the most difficult problem the Course addresses, which we will talk about a little later: special relationships. It is very tempting to form a special relationship with the Course and to make it something really special in a negative sense. When we talk about special relationships later this will become clearer.

Chapter 2

ONE-MINDEDNESS:
THE WORLD OF HEAVEN

One helpful way, perhaps, of presenting the material in *A Course in Miracles* is to break it up into three sections, since the Course really represents three different thought systems: One-mindedness, which represents the world of Heaven; wrong-mindedness, which represents the thought system of the ego; and right-mindedness, which represents the thought system of the Holy Spirit.

It is also helpful at the beginning to notice that *A Course in Miracles* is written on two levels (see the chart on the next page). The first level presents the difference between the One Mind and the split mind, while the second level contrasts wrong- and right-mindedness. On the first level, for example, the world and the body are regarded as illusions made by the ego. They thus symbolize the separation from God.

The second level relates to this world where we believe we are, and so on this level, the world and the body are seen as neutral and can serve one of two purposes. To the wrong-minded ego, they are instruments used to reinforce separation. To the right mind, they

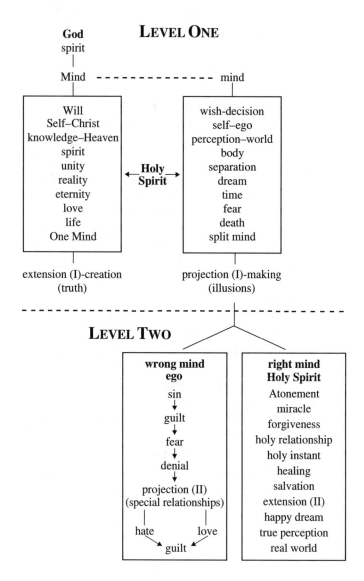

are the Holy Spirit's teaching devices, through which we learn His lessons of forgiveness. On this second level, therefore, illusions refer to the misperceptions of the ego; for example seeing attack instead of a call for love, sin instead of error.

With this in mind, then, let us begin our discussion of the three thought systems of the Course. We will start with the first one, which in reality is the only one, and is described at the beginning of the text as the One-mindedness of Christ or of God. This is a thought system that has nothing to do with this world. I will talk about it briefly now and then we will set it aside, because in effect this is not the main thrust of the Course. It is the underpinning of it and the foundation for it, but it is really not where the work has to be done.

One-mindedness is the world of Heaven, what *A Course in Miracles* refers to as knowledge. One of the difficult things, when you come to the Course for the first time, is that it will use words differently from the way that we use them in ordinary speech. If you superimpose your own understanding of a word on the Course, you will have a lot of trouble. Words such as "sin," "world," "reality," "God," "Jesus," "knowledge," etc., are used slightly differently from the way we use them ordinarily. If you are going to do justice to the Course and understand what it is saying, whether you agree with it or not, you must also understand the meaning of the words and how it uses them within its own context.

One of these words is "knowledge." The Course does not use "knowledge" as we typically use it. Knowledge refers only to God, and the world of knowledge has nothing to do with this world. Knowledge is not a belief or a system of thought. It is an experience, and an experience that wholly transcends anything of this world. So the world of Heaven, the world of knowledge, or God's world of spirit, are all the same. When *A Course in Miracles* speaks of the world of spirit, this has nothing to do with the world of matter. Spirit is our true reality, our true home, and again has nothing to do with what we experience as our reality here.

The central concept in Heaven, or the world of knowledge, is the Trinity. I will talk briefly about how the Course defines Trinity, but first let me talk about one other thing, and that is an objection that many people raise about the Course. They will ask: If the Course's theme and general thought is of a universal nature—that we are all one—then why did it come in a specifically Christian form?

The answer to this makes sense in light of one of the fundamental principles of the Course: You must undo error where it is found. There is no question that the most dominant influence in the Western world is Christianity. There has not been a more powerful system of thought in the world, whether you identify yourself as a Christian or not. There is no one in this world, certainly in the Western world, who has not been profoundly affected by Christianity. Whether or not we identify with Christianity, we do live in a Christian world. Our very calendar is based on the birth and death of Jesus. However, Christianity has not been very Christian, which also goes without saying, as we look at the history of the Churches.

Because Christianity has had such a powerful impact on the world, and still does—and it has not been a very Christian impact—it was essential that the errors of Christianity be undone first, before anything else could be done to radically change the thought system of the world. That is why, I believe, *A Course in Miracles* came in the specifically Christian form it did. So anyone who reads through the Course and has had a Christian background will recognize rather early on that the Christianity that the Course talks about has nothing to do with the Christianity that he or she was taught. Helen's husband, Louis, a man very much identified with Judaism, said to me once that he knows that if Christianity had been like the Course, there never would have been any anti-Semitism. There is no question about that.

The Course, therefore, came in the form that it did to correct the errors that Christianity has introduced. Throughout the Course, especially in the early chapters

29

of the text, there are numerous references to scripture (more than 800), and many of them have been reinterpreted. The beginnings of Chapters 3 and 6 have very powerful sections on the crucifixion where Jesus sets the record straight, explaining what went wrong in terms of how people understood his crucifixion (T-3.I; T-6.I). He explains why that happened and how a whole system of thought evolved out of that mistake. Jesus' discussion is not traditionally Christian, though its principles are Christian in the sense of how he originally meant them.

That is why *A Course in Miracles* is Christian in its form, and why several times throughout the text Jesus says that he needs us to forgive him. This applies whether you are Christian, Jew, or atheist. There is no one in this world who, on one level or another, consciously or otherwise, has not made Jesus into an enemy. The reason for that is the same reason people find his Course to be an enemy. He threatens the very foundation of the ego system. So once again, before we can move beyond what Christianity has been, we first have to forgive it. Again, this will be in full keeping with the principles of the Course.

The fact that the Course uses Christian terminology has been a stumbling block for practically everyone who reads it. It is an obvious stumbling block for those people brought up as Jews, because as a Jew you are taught very early on that "Jesus" is a negative word. It is a stumbling block for most Christians because the Course expresses a form of Christianity that is different from the Christianity they had known. For a person who is an atheist, there obviously are problems too. Again, there is practically no one who will not experience some difficulty with *A Course in Miracles* because of its form. Therefore, the fact that it is Christian is deliberate; the fact that Jesus makes no secret of the fact he is the author of the Course also is no accident. The purpose is really to help the world to forgive him and to forgive itself for its misinterpretations.

Q: What about the poetry?

A: Helen was a Shakespearean buff and the iambic pentameter that is found in much of the Course is Shakespearean in style. There are also several allusions to Shakespeare's plays, and the version of the Bible that is quoted is the King James version. However, while there are some striking parallels with the teachings of the Bible, the Course, as I have said, really differs from what we might call biblical Christianity.

One final point: because of its purpose of correcting Christianity, the Course deliberately uses Christian words for the Trinity, which are masculine words. This is another objection many people have raised against the Course. The reason for this usage is twofold. One is that the language of Judaism and Christianity has been masculine and the Course just adopts that; a second reason is that so much of it is written in poetic form that to always have to say "his or her" would be a little cumbersome. That is part of the limitations of English grammar. For example, if you make reference to a person and in the next sentence you want to refer back to that person with a pronoun, to be grammatically correct you must use the masculine gender. That is a stylistic aspect of the English language and the Course simply goes along with that. I can assure you that the author of the Course is not a sexist; Jesus is not a male chauvinist.

The first Person of the Trinity, of course, is God. God is the Source of all being. He is frequently referred to in the Course as the Father, which again is clearly taken from the Judaeo-Christian tradition. He is referred to also as the Creator, and everything comes from Him. God's nature, in essence, is pure spirit, and because God is changeless, formless, eternal, and spirit, nothing that does not share in those attributes can be real. That is why the Course says the world is not real, and was not created by God. The world is changeable; it is not eternal and it is material form. Therefore, it cannot be of God.

The second Person of the Trinity is Christ. What happened in creation is that God just naturally extended Himself. The natural state of spirit is to extend and flow. The extension of God is creation, and creation is known as God's Son, or Christ. What is difficult to understand about this is that the only words or concepts that we can use are those of our own world, a world of perception, which is limited by time and space. This is the material universe we made up as the substitute for Heaven. Elaboration of this is beyond the scope of this one-day workshop, however.

In Heaven, therefore, there is no time or space. When we think of God extending Himself, the only image we can have is a temporal and spatial one, which would not be accurate. As the Course says on those occasions, do not even try to understand something that cannot be understood. The workbook uses the phrase "senseless musings" (W-pI.139.8:5), and that is really what all of this is. As *A Course in Miracles* states, only through a revelatory experience can we apprehend truth, and then we could not possibly put that into words: words are but symbols of symbols—therefore they are twice removed from the state of reality (M-21.1:9-10).

Now God's Son, or Christ, also extends Himself. The extension of God is His Son, and He is called Christ. Christ is one: There is only one God, and only one Son. In other words, similar to what God does in extending His spirit, God's Son also does in extending His spirit. This leads us to one of the most ambiguous terms in the Course: "creations." When the Course refers to creations, what it is referring to are the extensions of Christ's spirit. Just as God created Christ, Christ also creates. And the extensions of Christ in Heaven are known as creations. This is an area which the Course does not attempt to explain. When you come across this word, it is sufficient to realize that it just signifies the natural process of extension of spirit.

A Course in Miracles makes it very clear, and this is a very important point, that while we, as Christ, create as God, we did not create God. We are not God. We are extensions of God; we are God's Sons but we are not the Source. There is only one Source and that is God. To believe that we are God, that we are the Source of being, is to do exactly what the ego wants, and that is to believe that we are autonomous and that we can create God, just as God has created us. If you believe this, you are setting up a closed circle from which there is no way out, because then you are saying that you are the author of your own reality. That is what the Course refers to as the authority problem. We are not the author of our reality; God is. Once we believe that we are God, we are setting ourselves up in competition with Him, and then we really have trouble. That, of course, is what the original error is, which we will talk about in a little while.

In the beginning, which of course transcends time, there was only God and His Son. It was like one big happy family in Heaven. At some strange moment, which in reality never happened, the Son of God believed that he could separate himself from his Father. That is the moment when the separation occurred. In truth, as the Course says, this could never have happened, because how could a part of God separate itself from God? Yet the fact that we are all here, or we think we are here, would seem to indicate something else. The Course does not really explain the separation; it just says that this is how it is. Do not try to ask how the impossible could have happened, because it could not have happened. If you ask how it could have happened, you are right back in the middle of the error.

In our own way of thinking, it did seem to happen and a separation did occur. That same instant that we believed we separated ourselves from God, we set up a whole new thought system (which I will talk about in just a minute) and God sent His Correction to undo this mistake. He is the third Person of the Trinity. This is explained very well in Chapter 5 of the text if you want to study this further. It is the first place where Jesus talks specifically about the Holy Spirit and explains the Holy Spirit's role: He is the Answer to the separation. Wherever in the Course you read the word "Answer" with a capital "A," you can substitute "Holy Spirit."

A Course in Miracles describes the Holy Spirit as the Communication Link between God and His separated Son (T-6.I.19:1). The reason that He is the Answer and undoes the separation is that since we

actually believe that we are separate from God—
God is there and we are here—the Holy Spirit acts as
a link between where we believe we are and where
we truly are, which is back with God. The fact that
there is a link tells us that we are not separated. So at
the moment we believed that there was a separation,
at that same instant God undid it. And so the undoing
of the separation is the Holy Spirit.

Now again, that is the thought system known as
One-mindedness, and it is the underpinning of everything else that we will talk about. It is not anything
that can be understood; it just has to be accepted.
When we are all back in Heaven we will understand
it, and then we will not have any questions.

Chapter 3

WRONG-MINDEDNESS:
THE THOUGHT SYSTEM OF THE EGO

The two thought systems critical for understanding *A Course in Miracles* are wrong-mindedness and right-mindedness. As I have mentioned earlier, wrong-mindedness can be equated with the ego. Right-mindedness can be equated with the thought system of the Holy Spirit, which is forgiveness. The ego's thought system is not a very happy one. As the Course makes very clear, the thought systems of both the ego and the Holy Spirit are perfectly logical and consistent within themselves. They are also mutually exclusive. But it is very helpful to understand exactly what the logic of the ego system is, because it *is* very logical. And once you get that logical sequence, it will make very clear a lot of the things in the text which otherwise seem obscure.

One of the difficulties in studying *A Course in Miracles* is that it is not like other thought systems. Most thought systems proceed in a linear way where you begin with simple ideas that build upon themselves and get more complex. The Course is not like that. The Course's thought system is presented in a circular fashion. It seems to go around and around the same material over and over again. Think of an image of a well: You go around and around the well as you get deeper and deeper until you get to the bottom. And the bottom of this well would be God. But you keep going around the same circle. It is just that as you get deeper you get closer to the bedrock of the ego system. But it is always the same thing. And that is why the text says the same thing over and over again. Because it is almost impossible to get it the first time or the hundredth time, you need the six hundred and twenty-two pages.* It is a process, and this is one of the things that distinguishes *A Course in Miracles* from any other spiritual system. While it is presented as a very intellectualized thought system, it really is an experiential process. It is deliberately written the way it is from the pedagogic point of view of not having us study it as we would any other system, but rather to have us be led around this well. In the process of working through the material of the Course, and working through the material of our personal lives, we will increasingly understand what the Course says. Nonetheless, I do think it is helpful to go through the ego's thought system from a linear point of view, so we can understand how it is built up. This will make it easier as we read through the pages of the text.

---

* There are 669 pages in the text in the second edition.

Sin, Guilt, and Fear

There are three key ideas in understanding the ego's thought system. These are the foundation blocks of the whole system and they are sin, guilt, and fear. Whenever you see the word "sin" in the Course you can always substitute the word "separation," because the two words are the same. The sin that we are most guilty of, which ultimately is the source of all our guilt, is the sin of our belief in a separation from God, the topic I described just a minute ago. This is roughly the same as what the Churches have taught as "original sin." The description in the third chapter of Genesis gives a perfect account of how the ego was born. In fact, it is referred to in the first section of Chapter 2 in the text (T-2.I.3-4).

So the beginning of the ego is the belief that we have separated ourselves from God. This is what sin is: the belief that we have separated ourselves from our Creator and have set up a self that is separate from our true Self. The Self is synonymous with Christ. Wherever you see the capitalized word "Self," you can substitute the word "Christ."

We believe that we have established a self (with a little "s") that is our true identity, and this self is autonomous from our real Self and from God. This is the beginning of all of the trouble in the world: the belief that we are individuals separate from God. Once we believe that we have committed this sin, or once we believe that we have committed any sin, it is psychologically inevitable that we will then feel guilty over what we believe we have done. In some sense, guilt may be defined as the experience of having sinned. So we can basically use sin and guilt synonymously: Once we believe that we have sinned, it is impossible that we not believe we are guilty and feel what is known as guilt.

When *A Course in Miracles* talks about guilt, it uses the word differently from how it is usually used, which almost always is to connote that I feel guilty for what I have done or have not done. Guilt is always attached to specific things from our past. But these conscious experiences of guilt are only like the tip of an iceberg. If you think of an iceberg, beneath the surface of the sea is this huge mass that would represent what guilt is. Guilt is really the sum total of all the negative feelings, beliefs, and experiences that we have ever had about ourselves. So guilt can be any form of self-hatred or self-rejection: feelings of incompetence, failure, emptiness, or feelings that there are things in us that are lacking or missing or incomplete.

Most of this guilt is unconscious; that is why the image of an iceberg is so helpful. Most of these experiences of just how rotten we really believe we are lie beneath the surface of our conscious mind which, of course, makes them virtually inaccessible to us. And the ultimate source of all this guilt is the belief that we have sinned against God by separating ourselves from Him. As a result of that, then, we see ourselves as separate from everybody else and from our Self.

Once we feel guilty, it is impossible not to believe that we will be punished for the terrible things that we believe we have done and the terrible thing that we believe we are. As the Course teaches, guilt will always demand punishment. Once we feel guilty, we will believe that we must be punished for our sins. Psychologically there is no way of avoiding that step. We will then be afraid. All fear, no matter what its seeming cause in the world, comes from the belief that I should be punished for what I have done or for what I have not done. And I will then be afraid of what this punishment will be.

Because we believe that the ultimate object of our sin is God, against Whom we have sinned by separating from Him, we will then believe that it will be God Himself Who will punish us. As you read through the Bible and come across all of those terrible passages about the wrath and vengeance of God, this is where they come from. It has nothing to do with God as He is, since God is only Love. It has everything to do, however, with the projections of our own guilt onto Him. It was not God Who cast Adam and Eve out of the Garden of Eden; it was Adam and Eve who cast themselves out of the Garden of Eden.

Once we believe that we have sinned against God, which we all do, we must also believe that God will punish us. The Course talks about the four obstacles to peace, and the last obstacle is the fear of God (T-19.IV-D). What we have done, of course, is that by becoming afraid of God we have changed the God of Love into a God of fear: a God of hatred, punishment, and vengeance. This is just what the ego wants us to do. Once we feel guilt, no matter what we believe the guilt is from, we are also believing that not only are we guilty, but that God is going to strike us dead. So God, Who is our loving Father and our only Friend, becomes our enemy. And He is quite an enemy to have, needless to say. Once again, this is the origin of all the beliefs that you read in the Bible or anywhere else about God being a punishing Father. To believe that He is, is to attribute to Him the same ego qualities that we have. As Voltaire said, "God created man in His own image, and then man returned the compliment." The God we created is really the image of our own ego.

No one can exist in this world with that degree of fear and terror, and with that degree of self-hatred and guilt in his or her conscious mind. It would be absolutely impossible for us ever to live with that amount of anxiety and terror; it would just devastate us. There has to be some way, therefore, that we can cope with this. Since it is not God that we can go to for help, because within the ego system we have already turned God into an enemy, the only other recourse available to us is the ego itself.

We go to the ego for help and say: "Look, you have got to do something; I cannot tolerate all this anxiety and terror that I feel. Help!" The ego, true to its form, does give us help which is not really help at all, though it appears to be. The "help" comes in two basic forms, and it is really here that the contributions of Freud can be truly understood and appreciated.

Denial and Projection

I think I should put a little plug in for Freud, who gets a bad press these days. People are big on Jung as well as other non-traditional psychologists, and rightly so, but Freud gets shoved to the background. However, the basic understanding of the ego in the Course is directly based on Freud's teachings. He was a very brilliant man, and if it were not for Freud there would not have been *A Course in Miracles*. Jung himself said, for all of the problems that he had with Freud, that he was merely standing on Freud's shoulders. And that is true for anybody who has come since Freud. Freud very systematically and logically described exactly how the ego functions.

3. WRONG-MINDEDNESS: THE EGO

Let me just mention that Freud uses the word "ego" in a different way from how the Course does. In the Course, "ego" is used as a rough equivalent to the usage of the East. In other words, the ego is the self with a small "s." For Freud, the ego is only one part of the psyche, which consists of the id (the unconscious), the superego (the conscience), and the ego, which is the part of the mind that integrates all of this. The ways the Course uses the word "ego" would be roughly equivalent to the total Freudian psyche. You just have to make that transition to work with the Course.

Freud's one mistake incidentally was a whopper! He did not recognize that the entire psyche was a defense against our true Self, our true reality. Freud was so afraid of his own spirituality that he had to construct a thought system that was virtually impregnable to the threat of spirit. And he really did just that. But he was absolutely brilliant in describing how the psyche or the ego works. His mistake, again, was in not recognizing that the whole thing was a defense against God. Basically what we are talking about today in terms of the ego is based on what Freud had said. We all really owe him a tremendous debt of gratitude. Particularly noteworthy were Freud's contributions in the area of the defense mechanisms, helping us to understand how we defend ourselves against all the guilt and fear that we have.

When we go to the ego for help, we open a book by Freud and find two things which will help very much. The first is repression, or denial. (The Course never uses the word "repression"; it uses the word "denial." But you can use either one.) What we do with this guilt, this sense of sin, and with all the terror that we feel, is make believe it is not there. We just push it down out of awareness, and this pushing down is known as repression or denial. We just deny its existence to ourselves. For example, if we are too lazy to sweep our floor we sweep the dirt under the carpet, and then make believe it is not there; or an ostrich who is frightened just sticks its head in the sand so that it does not have to deal with or look at what is so threatening to it. Well this does not work for obvious reasons. If we keep sweeping dirt under a carpet, it is going to make it very lumpy and we will eventually trip, while the ostrich could get badly hurt remaining in its head-down position.

But on some level we know that our guilt *is* there. So we go to the ego again and say that "denial was really fine, but you are going to have to do something else. This stuff is going to mount up and then I am going to explode. Please help me." And then the ego says, "I have just the thing for you." It tells us to look at page so-and-so in Freud's *Interpretation of Dreams*, or wherever, and there we will find what is known as projection. There is probably no single idea in *A Course in Miracles* that is more critical to understand than this. If you do not understand projection you will not understand a single word in the Course, either in terms of how the ego functions or how the Holy Spirit will undo what the ego has done. Projection very simply means that you take something from inside of you and say it really is not here; it is outside of me in someone else. The word itself literally means to throw out, or hurl away from or toward something else, and this is what we all do in projection. We take the guilt, or the sinfulness that we believe is inside of us, and we say: It is really not in me; it is in you. I am not the guilty person, you are the guilty person. I am not the one who is responsible for how miserable and unhappy I am; you are. From the standpoint of the ego it does not matter who the "you" is. The ego does not care whom you project onto as long as you find someone onto whom you could unload your guilt. This is how the ego tells us we get rid of our guilt.

About the best description of this process of projection that I know of is found in the Old Testament, in Chapter 16 of the Book of Leviticus, where the Children of Israel are told what they should do on the Day of Atonement, Yom Kippur. They are told to gather together, and in the center of the camp is Aaron who, as the High Priest, is the mediator between the people and God. Next to Aaron is a goat, and Aaron places his hand on the goat and symbolically transfers all the sins the people have accumulated over the year onto this poor goat. They then kick the goat out of camp. That is a perfect and graphic account of just what projection is and, of course, that is where we get the word "scapegoat."

Thus, we take our sins and say they are not in us; they are in you. And then we put distance between ourselves and our sins. Nobody wants to be near his sinfulness and so we take it from inside of ourselves and place it on someone else, and then we banish that person from our life. There are two basic ways to do that. One is to physically separate ourselves from another person; the other is to do it psychologically. The psychological separation is really the most devastating and also the most subtle.

The way that we separate ourselves from someone else, once we put our sins on them, is to attack them or get angry at them. Any expression of our anger—whether it is in the form of a mild twinge of annoyance or intense rage (it does not make any difference; they are all the same [W-pI.21.2:3-5])—is always an attempt to justify the projection of our guilt, no matter what our anger's cause seems to be. This need to project our guilt is the root cause of all anger. You do not have to agree with what other people say or do, but the minute you experience a personal response of anger, judgment, or criticism, it is always because you have seen in that other person something that you

have denied in yourself. In other words, you are projecting your own sin and guilt onto that person and
you attack it there. But this time you are not attacking
it in yourself; you are attacking it in that other person
and you want to get that person as far away from you
as possible. What you really want to do is get your sin
as far away from you as possible.

One of the interesting things when one reads the
Old Testament, especially Chapters 11 through 15 in
Leviticus, the third book of the Torah, is to see how
detailed the Children of Israel were in trying to identify the forms of uncleanliness that were around
them, and then how they should keep themselves separate from it. There are some quite detailed passages
that describe what uncleanliness is, whether it is in
qualities in people, forms of uncleanliness, or certain
people in and of themselves. Then it explains how the
children of Israel should be kept separate from those
forms of uncleanliness. Whatever other reasons may
have been involved, a key meaning of these teachings
was the psychological necessity to get your own uncleanliness from inside of you and place it outside in
someone else, and then separate yourself from that
person.

It is interesting when you have that understanding
to then go into the New Testament and see how Jesus
moved against that. All of the forms of uncleanliness
that people had defined and saw as essential to their

religion to keep separate, he embraced. The social out-casts that were defined by Jewish Law he went out of his way to embrace, as if to say, "You cannot project your guilt onto other people. You must identify it in yourself and heal it there." That is why the gospel says such things as you clean the inside of your cup, not the outside (Lk 11:39); do not be concerned with the beam in your brother's eye, be concerned with the mote in yours (Lk 6:41-42); and it is not what comes into a man that makes him unclean, it is what comes from in-side him (Mt 15:11). The point is exactly the same as in the Course: The source of our sinfulness is not out-side but inside. But projection seeks to have us see our sin outside of us and then to solve the problem there, and so we never really see that the problem is inside.

When we go to the ego for help and say, "Help me get rid of my guilt," the ego says, "Okay, the way you get rid of your guilt is you first repress it, and then you project it onto other people. That is how you get rid of your guilt." What the ego does not tell us is that pro-jected guilt is an attack and the best way to hold on to the guilt. The ego is nobody's fool; it wants to keep us guilty. Let me explain this idea for a moment because it is also one of the key ideas for understanding how the ego counsels us.

A Course in Miracles speaks of "the attraction of guilt" (T-19.IV-A.10-17). The ego is very attracted to feeling guilty, and its reason is obvious once you remember what the ego is. The ego's rationale for its advice to deny and project is based on the following: The ego is nothing more than a belief, and it is a belief in the reality of the separation. The ego is the false self that seemingly came into being when we separated ourselves from God. Therefore as long as we believe that the separation is real the ego is in business. Once we believe that there is no separation, then the ego is finished. As the Course would say, the ego, with the world it made, disappears back into the nothingness from which it came (M-13.1:2). The ego really is nothing. As long as we believe that original sin occurred, that the sin of separation is real, then we are saying that the ego is real. What teaches us that sin is real is guilt. Any feeling of guilt is always a statement that says, "I have sinned." And the ultimate meaning of sin is that I have separated myself from God. Therefore as long as I believe that my sin is real, I am guilty. Whether I see the guilt in me or in another person I am saying that sin is real and that the ego is real. The ego therefore has a vested interest in keeping us guilty.

Any time the ego is confronted with guiltlessness it will attack it, because the greatest sin against the ego's thought system is to be guiltless. If you are guiltless you are also sinless, and if you are sinless there is no ego. There is a line in the text that says: "To the ego, *the guiltless are guilty*" (T-13.II.4:2), because

50

to be guiltless is to sin against the ego's command-ment: "Thou shalt be guilty." If you are guiltless, you are then guilty of being guiltless. That, for example, is why the world killed Jesus. He was teaching us that we are guiltless, and therefore it had to kill him be-cause he was blaspheming against the ego.

Therefore the ego's fundamental purpose always is to keep us guilty. But it cannot tell us that because if it does, we are not going to pay any attention to it. So the ego tells us that if we follow what it says, we will be free of our guilt. And the way to do that, again, is to deny its presence in ourselves, see it in someone else, and then attack that person. That way we will be free of our guilt. But what it does not tell us is that attack is the best way to *stay* guilty. This is true because, as an-other psychological axiom states, whenever you attack anyone, either in your own mind or in actuality, you will feel guilty. There is no way you could hurt any-one, whether in thought or in deed, without feeling guilty. You may not experience the guilt—for ex-ample, psychopaths do not experience their guilt—but that does not mean that on a deeper level you do not feel guilty.

What the ego does then, very cleverly, is set up a cycle of guilt and attack, whereby the more guilty we feel, the greater will be our need to deny it in ourselves and attack someone else for it. But the more we attack someone else, the greater will be our guilt over what we have done, because at some level we will recognize that we have attacked that person falsely. That will only make us feel guilty, and this will keep the whole thing going around and around. It is this cycle of guilt and attack that makes this world go around; it is not love. If anyone tells you that love makes this world go around, then he does not know very much about the ego. Love is of God's world and it is possible to *reflect* that love in this world. In this world, however, love has no place. What *does* have a place is guilt and attack, and it is this dynamic which is so present in our own lives, individually as well as collectively.

The Attack-Defense Cycle

A secondary cycle that gets set up is the attack-defense cycle. Once I believe that I am guilty and I project my guilt onto you and attack you, I will then believe (because of the principle I mentioned earlier) that my guilt will demand punishment. Because I have attacked you I will believe that I am deserving of being attacked back. Now whether you actually attack or not really does not matter; I will believe that you are going to do it because of my own guilt. Believing that you are going to attack me back, I will then believe that I must defend myself against your attack. And since I am trying to deny the fact that I am guilty,

I will feel that your attack against me is unjustified. The moment that I attack you, my unconscious fear is that you are going to attack me back, and I had better be prepared for that. So I have to build up a defense against your attack. All that this will do is make you fearful, and then we reach a partnership on this, where the more I attack you, the more you have to defend yourself against me and attack me back, and I will have to defend myself against you and attack you back. And we will go back and forth (W-pI.153.2-3).

This dynamic, of course, is what explains the insanity of the nuclear arms race. It also explains the insanity that we all feel. The greater my need to defend myself, the more I am reinforcing the very fact that I am guilty. This is also a very important principle to understand in terms of the ego, and it is stated probably most clearly in a line from the text that says, "Defenses *do* what they would defend" (T-17.IV.7:1). The purpose of all defenses is to protect or defend ourselves against our fear. If I were not afraid, I would not have to have a defense, but the very fact that I need a defense is telling me that I should be fearful, because if I were not fearful I would not have to bother with a defense. The very fact that I am defending myself is reinforcing the fact that I should be afraid and I should be afraid because I am guilty. So the very thing that my defenses are supposed to protect me from—my fear—they are reinforcing. Therefore, the more that I defend myself, the more I am teaching myself that I am an ego: sinful, guilty, and fearful.

The ego really is nobody's fool. It convinces us that we have to defend ourselves, but the more we do that the guiltier we feel. It tells us in many different ways how we should defend ourselves against our guilt. But the very protection that it offers will reinforce this guilt. That is why we go spinning around and around and around. There is a wonderful lesson that says, "In my defenselessness my safety lies" (W-pI.153). If I am going to truly know that I am safe and that my true protection is God, the best way for me to do that is not to defend myself. That is why we read in the gospels of Jesus' last days where he did not defend himself at all. From the moment that he was arrested, throughout all the time he was being mocked, scourged, persecuted, and even killed, he did not defend himself (see, for example, Mt 26:52-53 and Mt 27:14). And what he was saying was, "I do not need a defense" for, as it says in the workbook, "the Son of God needs no defense against the truth of his reality" (W-pI.135.26:8). When we truly know Who we are and know Who our Father is, our Father in Heaven, we do not have to protect ourselves because truth needs no defense. However, within the ego system we will feel that we need protection and thus we will always defend ourselves. So these two cycles really act to keep the whole ego business going. The guiltier we feel, the more we will attack. The more we attack, the guiltier we will feel. The more we attack, the more we will feel the need to defend ourselves from our expected punishment or counterattack, which is in itself an attack.

The second chapter of Genesis ends with Adam and Eve standing naked before each other, without shame. Shame is really just another word for guilt, and shamelessness is an expression of the pre-separation condition. In other words, there was no guilt because there had been no sin. It is the third chapter where original sin is talked about, and that begins with Adam and Eve eating of the forbidden fruit. The act of doing that constitutes their disobedience with God, and that really is the sin. In other words, they see themselves as having a will that is separate from God and that can choose something different from what God has created. And that again is the birth of the ego: the belief that sin is possible. So they eat of the fruit, and the very first thing they do after that is look at each other—and this time they do feel shame and cover themselves. They put fig leaves around their sexual organs and this then becomes an expression of their guilt. They realize that they have done something sinful and the nakedness of their bodies becomes the symbol of their sin. So that has to be defended against, and that expresses their guilt.

The very next thing that follows is that Adam and Eve hear the voice of God, Who is looking for them, and they now become afraid of what God will do if He catches them. So they hide in the bushes so God will not see them. Right there you see the connection of the belief in sin—that you can separate yourself from God—with the feeling of guilt of having done so, and then the fear of what will happen when God catches up with us and punishes us. Indeed, as the third chapter continues, Adam and Eve were absolutely right, because God does punish them. The interesting thing is that when God does finally confront Adam, he projects the guilt onto Eve and says "I am not the one who did it, it was Eve who made me do it." (It is always the woman who gets it.) And so God looks at Eve, who does the very same thing and says, "I am not the one who did it. Do not blame me, it was the serpent." Thus we see exactly what we do to defend ourselves from our fear and our guilt: We project the blame onto someone else.

Remember what I said earlier: Guilt will always demand punishment. The ego will demand that Adam and Eve be punished for their sin, so that when God does catch up with them He punishes them with a life filled with pain and suffering, from the moment of birth through the end, which is death. At the end of the day, I will talk about how Jesus undoes this whole process. At any rate, that chapter in Genesis is a

56

perfect summary of the whole structure of the ego: the relationship among sin, guilt, and fear.

One of the major ways the ego defends against guilt is to attack other people, and that is what our anger always seems to do: justify the projection of our guilt onto others. It is extremely important to recognize just how strong an investment the world has, and each of us has as part of the world, in justifying the fact that we are angry, because we all need to have an enemy. There is no one in this world who on some level or another does not invest the world with properties of good and bad. And we separate the world and put some people in the good category and some in the bad. The purpose of this is our tremendous need to have someone that we can project our guilt onto. We need at least one person, or one idea or group, that we can make into the bad one, into the scapegoat. This is the source of all prejudice and discrimination. It is the tremendous need that we have, which is usually unconscious, to find someone that we can make the scapegoat so that we can escape from the burden of our own guilt. This has been the case from the beginning of recorded history. It has been the case of every major system of thought, or system of living that has ever existed in the world. It is always predicated on the basis that there are good guys and bad guys.

You can certainly see this in the history of Christianity itself. Right from the beginning there was the process of separating out the good from the bad: The Jews who believed in Jesus against the Jews who did not believe in Jesus, and then those who did believe in Jesus separated into the followers of St. Peter, St. Paul, St. James, etc., and the Church has been subdividing ever since. This is so because of the same unconscious need to find someone that we can see as being different and not as good as ourselves. Again, it is extremely helpful for us to recognize how strong an investment we have in that process. That is why at a movie everyone cheers at the end when the good guy wins and the bad guy loses. We share the same investment in seeing the bad guy being punished, because at that point we believe that we have escaped from our sins.

Special Relationships

What I have been describing up to now in terms of anger is really only one form that projection takes. It is the most obvious of the two forms of attack that are referred to in the Course as special relationships. The most difficult concept to understand in the Course, and even more difficult to actually live and put into practice, is the idea of specialness and the turning of our special relationships into holy ones.

Special relationships come in two forms. The first is special hate relationships—which we have been talking about—where we find someone whom we make the object of our hate so that we may escape the true object of our hate, which is ourself. The second form is what the Course refers to as special love relationships. These are the most powerful and insidious because they are the most subtle. And again, there is no more difficult concept in the Course to understand or to apply to oneself than this one. Special relationships are not mentioned in the workbook or the manual at all, and do not appear in the text until Chapter 15, and from then on, for about the next nine chapters, that is almost all you read about.

The reason that special love is so difficult to recognize and do something about is that it seems to be something that it is not. It is very difficult to conceal from yourself the fact that you are angry at someone. You can do so for a while, but it is really hard to maintain that illusion for too long. Special love is quite something else. It always will seem to be what it is not. It really is the most tempting and deceptive phenomenon in this world. It basically follows the same principles as special hate, but it does so in a different form. The basic principle is that we attempt to get rid of our guilt by seeing it in someone else. Therefore, it is really just a thinly disguised veil over hatred. Hatred, again, is only an attempt to hate someone else so we do not have to experience our true hatred of ourself. What I would like to do now is show basically how this works in three different ways —how in the guise of saving us from our guilt through "love," the ego is really reinforcing its guilt through hatred.

Let me first describe what special love is, and then we will talk about how it operates. If you recall, right at the beginning when I was talking about guilt and going through the list of words that comprise guilt, one of the expressions that I used was the belief that there is something missing in us, that we have a certain lack. This is what the Course refers to as the "scarcity principle," and it really underlies the whole dynamic of special love.

What the scarcity principle says is that there is something missing inside of us. There is something that is unfulfilled and incomplete. Because of this lack there are certain needs that we have. And this is an important part of the whole experience of guilt. So once again we turn to the ego and we say, "Help! This feeling of my nothingness or my emptiness, or this feeling of something missing, is absolutely intolerable; you have to do something." The ego says, "Okay, here is what we will do." And first, the ego slaps us in the face by saying, "Yes, you are absolutely right; you are just a miserable creature and there is absolutely nothing that can be done to change the fact that you are lacking and missing something that is vitally important for you." Of course the ego does not tell us that what is missing is God, because if the ego told us that, we would choose God and the ego would cease to exist. The ego says that there is something inherently missing in us and there is nothing that can be done to remedy that. But then it says there is something we *can* do about the pain of this lack. While it is true that there is nothing that can change this inherent lack in ourself, we can look outside of ourself for someone or something that can compensate for what is missing inside of us.

Basically, special love says that I have certain special needs that God cannot meet because, once again, I have unconsciously made God into an enemy, so I do not go to the true God for help within the ego system. But when I find you, a special person with certain special attributes or qualities, I decide you will meet my special needs. That is where the expression "special relationships" comes from. My special needs will be met by certain special qualities in you, and that makes you a special person. And when you meet my special needs as I have set them up, then I will love you. And then, when you have certain special needs that I can meet for you, you will love me. From the ego's point of view that is a marriage made in Heaven.

Therefore, what this world calls love is really specialness, a gross distortion of love as the Holy Spirit would see it. Another word which describes the same kind of dynamic is "dependency." I become dependent on you to meet my needs, and I will make you dependent on me to meet your needs. As long as we both do that, then everything is fine. Now that basically is what specialness is. Its intent is to compensate for the perceived lack in ourselves by using someone else to fill the gap. We do this most clearly and most destructively with people. However, we can also do it with substances and things. Someone, for example, who is an alcoholic is trying to fill up the emptiness in him- or herself through a special relationship with a bottle. People who overeat do the same thing. People who have some kind of mania to buy a lot of clothes, make a lot of money, acquire a lot of things, or have status in the world—it is all the same thing. It is an attempt to compensate for how rotten we feel about ourselves by doing something outside that will make us feel good. There is a very beautiful and powerful section near the end of the text, "Seek Not Outside Yourself" (T-29.VII). When we seek outside ourselves we are always seeking for an idol, which is defined as a substitute for God. It is really only God Who can meet this need. This is what specialness does then: It serves the ego's purpose of seeming to protect us from our guilt, but all the while it reinforces it. It does this in three basic ways which I will summarize now.

The first is that if I have this special need and you come along and meet it for me, then what I have really done is make you a symbol of my guilt. (I am talking now only within the ego's framework; let us not concern ourselves about the Holy Spirit for now.) What I have done is associate you with my guilt, because the only purpose that I have given my relationship and love for you is that it serve to meet my needs. Therefore, while on a conscious level I have made you a symbol of love, on an unconscious level what I have really done is make you into a symbol of my guilt. If I did not have this guilt, then I would not have this need for you. The very fact that I have this need for you is reminding me, unconsciously, that I am really guilty. So that is the first way that special love reinforces the very guilt its love is trying to defend against. The more important you become in my life, the more you will remind me that the real purpose you are serving in my life is to protect me from my guilt, which reinforces the fact that I am guilty.

A helpful image of this process is to imagine our mind as a glass jar, and in this jar is all of our guilt. What we want more than anything else in the world is to keep this guilt safely within the jar; we do not want to know about it. When we seek for a special partner, we are seeking for someone who will be a cover for this jar. We want that cover to be closed very tightly. As long as it is tight, my guilt cannot emerge in consciousness and therefore I will not know about it; it stays within my unconscious. The very fact that I need you to be a lid for my jar is reminding me that there is something terrible in that jar that I do not want to escape or get out. Once again, the very fact that I need you is reminding me, unconsciously, that I have all of this guilt.

The second way that special love reinforces guilt is the "Jewish mother syndrome." What happens when this person who has come along to meet all my needs suddenly starts to change and no longer meets my needs in quite the same way as he or she did in the beginning? Human beings have the unfortunate qualities of changing and growing; they do not stay fixed as we would want them to be. What this means, then, as the person begins to change (perhaps no longer needing me in the way that he or she needed me in the beginning) is that the lid on this jar will start to loosen. My special needs will no longer be met in the form that I had demanded. As this lid begins to loosen, my guilt suddenly starts to threaten me by coming to the surface and escaping. The guilt escaping from the jar would mean my becoming conscious of how terrible I really believe I am. And that is the experience that I will do anything in the world to avoid.

At one point in Exodus, God says to Moses, "No one can look on my face and live" (Ex 33:20). We can make the same statement about guilt: No one can look on the face of guilt and live. The experience of confronting just how terrible we really believe we are is so overwhelming that we would do anything in the world except deal with that. So when this lid starts loosening and my guilt starts to bubble up to the surface, I become panic-stricken because all of a sudden I am confronted with all these terrible feelings I have about myself. My goal then is very simple: to get that lid tightly screwed on again as fast as possible. This means that I want to get you to return to how you once were. There is no more powerful way in this world to get someone to do what you want than to make that person feel guilty. If you want anything done by anyone else, you make that person feel good and guilty and that person will do what you want. No one likes to feel guilty.

The manipulation through guilt is the Jewish mother's trademark. Everyone who is not Jewish also knows about this. You could be Italian, Irish, Polish, or whatever; it is the same thing because the syndrome is universal. What I am going to do is try to make you guilty and I will say something to this effect: "What happened to you? You used to be such a decent, kind, loving, thoughtful, sensitive, gentle, understanding person. Now look at you! Look how you have changed! Now you do not give a damn. You are selfish, self-seeking, insensitive," and on and on and on. What I am really trying to do is to get you to feel so guilty that you will go back to being the way that you used to be. Everyone knows about this, right?

Now if you are playing the same game of guilt that I am, you will do what I want and then the lid will get screwed tight again, and I will love you as I once did. If you do not, and you no longer play this game, then I will get good and angry with you and my love will very quickly turn to hate (which is what it was all the time). You always hate the one that you are dependent on for the reasons I gave in the first example, because the person you are so dependent on is reminding you of your guilt, which you hate. And therefore, by association, you will also hate the person you are professing to love. This second example shows this to be what it really is. When you no longer meet my needs as I need them to be met, I will start hating you. And the reason that I will hate you is that I cannot stand to deal with my own guilt. That is what is known as the ending of the honeymoon. In these days it seems to happen faster and faster.

When the special needs no longer are met in the way that they used to be, then the love turns to hate. What happens when the other person says that I will no longer be the lid on your jar is very obvious. Then

I find someone else. As one of the workbook lessons states: "Another can be found" (W-pI.170.8:7), and rather easily. Then you just shift the same dynamics from one person to another. You can do this repeatedly, over and over again, or until you do something with your real problem, which is your own guilt.

When you really let that guilt go, then you are ready to enter into a relationship that will be different. This will be love as the Holy Spirit sees it. But until you do that, and your only goal is to keep your guilt hidden, you just look for another lid on the jar. And the world is always very cooperative in finding people who will meet this need for us. And we just enter into a whole series of special relationships one after another, a process the Course describes in very painful detail.

The third way in which specialness is a disguise for hatred, and for guilt rather than love, holds for both special hate and special love. Whenever we use people as a vehicle to meet our own needs, we are really not seeing them for who they are; we are really not seeing the Christ in them. Rather, we are only interested in manipulating them so that they will meet our own needs. We are really not seeing them for the light that shines in them; we are really seeing them for the particular form of darkness that will correspond to our particular form of darkness. And whenever we use or manipulate anyone to meet our needs, we are really attacking them because we are attacking their true Identity as Christ, seeing them as an ego which reinforces the ego in ourselves. Attack is always hatred, and so we must feel guilty for having done so.

Thus, these three ways are exactly how the ego will reinforce guilt, even though it tells us it is doing something else. That is why the Course describes the special relationship as the home of guilt.

Again, what makes special love such a devastating and effective defense from the ego's point of view is that it seems to be something that it is not. It seems to be such a wonderful, loving, and holy thing when special love first happens. How quickly it can change, however, unless we are able to get beyond what it seems to be and get to the basic problem which is our guilt.

There is an important section in the text called "The Two Pictures" (T-17.IV), which describes the difference between the ego's picture and the Holy Spirit's picture. The ego's picture is special love and is a picture of guilt, suffering, and ultimately death. This is not the picture the ego wants us to see because, again, if we really knew what the ego was up to we would not pay attention to it. So the ego puts its picture within a very beautiful and ornate frame, which glitters with diamonds and rubies and all kinds of fancy jewels. We are seduced by the frame, or the seemingly good feelings that specialness is going to give us, and we do not recognize the real gift of guilt and death. It is only when we get close to the frame and really look at it, that we see that the diamonds are really tears and the rubies are drops of blood. This is what the ego is all about. This is a very powerful section. On the other hand, the Holy Spirit's picture is quite different. The Holy Spirit's frame is very loose, and drops away and lets us see the real gift, which is the Love of God.

There is another quality which is very important, and which always is a dead giveaway as to whether we are involved in a relationship that is a special one or are involved in a relationship that is a holy one. We can always tell this by our attitude toward other people. If we are involved in a special relationship, that relationship will be an exclusive one. There will be no room in it for anyone else. The reason for this is obvious once you recognize how the ego is really working. If I have made you into my savior, and what you are saving me from is my guilt, then that means that your love for me and the attention that you give me will save me from this guilt that I am trying to keep hidden. But if you start to have an interest that is not me—whether it is in another person or another activity—you will not give me one hundred percent of your attention. To whatever degree you start to shift your interest or attention to something or someone else, to that degree there is less that I will get. This means that if I do not get one hundred percent, this lid on my jar is going to start loosening. And that is the source of all jealousy. The reason that people get jealous is that they feel their special needs will no longer be met in the way that they were supposed to have been met.

Therefore if you love someone else in addition to me, that means that I am going to get less love. To the ego, love is quantitative. There is only a certain amount that goes around, so if I love this one then I cannot love that one as much. To the Holy Spirit, love is qualitative and embraces all people. This does not mean that we love everyone in the same way; that is not possible in this world. What it does mean, however, is that the source of the love is the same; the love itself is the same, but the means of expression will be different.

I will "love" my parents "more" than I will love the parents of anyone in this room, not in quality, but in quantity. The love will basically be the same but, obviously, will be expressed in a different way. It does not mean that because I love *my* parents I love *yours* less, or that my parents are better than yours. All that it means is that these are the people that I have chosen, for in my relationship with them I shall learn forgiveness, which allows me to remember God's Love. It does not mean that you should feel guilty if you have a deeper relationship with some people than with others. There are very clear examples of that in the gospels, where Jesus was closer with certain disciples than with others, and was closer with his disciples than with others of his followers. It does not mean that he loved any of the people less, but that the expression of the love was more intimate and deep with some than with others. (See, for example, Mt 17:1-2; Jn 13:23-25.)

A holy relationship means that in loving one person, you are not excluding someone else; it is not done at anyone else's expense. Special love will *always* be at someone else's expense. It is always a love of comparison where certain people are compared with others; some are found wanting and some are found acceptable. Love in this world is not like that. You just recognize that certain people have been "given" to you and chosen by you so that you can learn and teach certain lessons; but that does not make that person better or worse than anyone else. That, again, is how you can always tell when a relationship is a special one as opposed to a holy one, by the degree to which it excludes other people.

Chapter 4

RIGHT-MINDEDNESS:
THE HOLY SPIRIT'S THOUGHT SYSTEM

There is a beautiful passage in *A Course in Miracles* where Jesus says that he has saved all our loving thoughts and has purified them of all errors (T-5.IV.8:3-4). All that he needs from us to make that our reality is to accept the fact that this is so. But we cannot do that if we are still holding onto our guilt. What I will talk about now is how the Holy Spirit gives us a perfect way of letting go of all this guilt.

Anger – Forgiveness

The Holy Spirit is very clever. As clever as the ego thinks it is, the Holy Spirit does it one better. He uses the very dynamic of projection that the ego has used to crucify us and keep us in the prison of guilt, and thus turns the tables on the ego. If you think of projection as a movie projector, imagine that I am going to be the movie projector and I have my own film of guilt that I am always playing through. What that means is that I people all of my world with my own guilt. I project the guilt from my film onto the screens of these people and then I see my own sin and guilt in everyone else.

The reason that I do that, again, is that I am following the ego's logic that this is the way to get rid of my guilt. Now, there is no way that I can deal with my own guilt all by myself. There is no way to look on the face of guilt and live; it is too devastating a thought. But the very thing that the ego has used to attack me by reinforcing my guilt in the guise of letting it go—this very mechanism of having my guilt be placed outside of me—also gives me the chance of letting my guilt go. Seeing in you the guilt that I cannot confront in myself gives me the opportunity of letting it go. And that is what forgiveness is, pure and simple. Forgiveness is the undoing of the projection of guilt.

Once again, my projecting the very guilt that I cannot deal with and release in myself onto this screen that is you, gives me the opportunity of looking at it and saying that now I can see it differently. The sins and guilt that I overlook and forgive in you are really the very same sins and guilt that I am holding myself responsible for. This, by the way, has to do with the *content* of the sin, not the *form*, which might be quite different. By forgiving it in you, what I am in effect doing is forgiving it in myself. This is the key idea in the whole Course. This is really what all those words are about. We project our guilt onto other people, and so when we choose to look at that person as the Holy Spirit would have us look—through Christ's vision—we are able then to reverse our thinking about ourselves.

What I have done is project my own darkness onto you so that the light of Christ in you is obscured. By making the decision to say you are not in darkness— you are really in light, which is the decision to let go of the darkness that I have placed on you—I am really making the very same statement about myself. I am saying that not only does the light of Christ shine in you but it also shines in me. And, in fact, it is the same light. That is what forgiveness is.

What this means, then, is that we should be grateful for every single person in our lives, especially those with whom we have the most trouble. The ones that we hate the most, that we find the most disagreeable, the most uncomfortable to be with, are the very ones that the Holy Spirit has "sent" to us and can use to show us that we can make another choice about the person we first were tempted to project our guilt onto. If they had not been on the film and screen of our lives, we would not know that this guilt is really in us. Therefore, we would not have the opportunity of letting it go. The only chance we ever have to forgive our guilt and to be free from it is to see it in someone else and to forgive it there. By forgiving it in that other person, we are forgiving it in ourselves. Once again, in those few lines is the sum and substance of *A Course in Miracles*.

Forgiveness, then, can be summarized briefly in three basic steps. The first step is recognizing that the problem is not out there on my screen. The problem is inside, in *my* film. The first step says that my anger is not justified, even though my anger always tells me that the problem is outside of me in you, and that you must change so that I do not have to change. Thus the first step says that the problem is not outside, the problem rather is inside me. The reason this step is so important is that God placed the Answer to the problem of separation inside of us; the Holy Spirit is not outside of us, the Holy Spirit is inside of us, in our minds. By maintaining that the problem is outside of us which projection always does, we are keeping the problem from the answer. This is exactly what the ego wants, because if the problem of the ego is answered by the Holy Spirit, then there is no more ego.

Thus, the ego is very devious and subtle in having us believe the problem is outside of us, whether it is in another person—our parents, teachers, friends, spouses, children, President—or in the stock market, the weather, even in God Himself. We are all very good at seeing the problem where it is not, so that the solution to the problem can be kept separate from it. Two workbook lessons that make this very clear are 79 and 80: "Let me recognize the problem so it can be solved" and "Let me recognize my problems have been solved." There is only one problem and that is the belief in separation itself, or the problem of guilt, and that is always internal, not outside. But the first step in forgiveness once again is to say the problem is not in you; the problem is in me. The guilt is not in you, the guilt is in myself. The problem is not on that screen I projected onto; it is rather in the film inside of me which is a film of guilt.

Now the second step, which is the most difficult one, the step that we would all do anything in the world to avoid, is to now deal with what this film is, which is our own guilt. That, once again, is why we all have such a strong investment in justifying and maintaining this anger and attack, and in seeing the world as split up into good and bad. As long as we do that we do not have to deal with this second step, which is to look at our own guilt and all our feelings of self-hatred.

In the first step, I say that my anger is a decision that I made to project my guilt. Now in the second step, I say that this very guilt itself also represents a decision. It represents a decision to see myself as guilty rather than as guiltless. I must acknowledge instead that I am a Son of God rather than a son of the ego, that my true Home is not in this world but rather that my true Home is in God. We cannot do this until we first look at our guilt and say this is not what we really are. We cannot say that until we first look upon someone else and say, "You are not what I made of you; you are really what God created."

There are some very powerful passages in the Course that deal with just how terrifying this step is. A misconception that people frequently have, especially when they look at *A Course in Miracles* for the first few times, is to think that this is all nice and easy. The Course is deceptive if you are not careful. On one level it talks about how simple it is; how we are all really "home in God, dreaming of exile" (T-10.I.2:1); how all this will be done in an instant if we just change our minds, etc. What happens is that we see these passages and we forget about all of the other ones which talk about the terror that this process will entail: the discomfort, resistance, and conflict that will come as we begin to take these steps to deal with our guilt.

No one can let go of the ego without dealing with one's own guilt and fear because that is what the ego is. Jesus said in the gospel: "Unless you take up your cross and follow me, you cannot be my disciples"

(Mt 10:38; Mk 8:34; Lk 14:27). That is what he is talking about. To take up one's cross is to deal with one's own guilt and fear, transcending the ego. There is no way that one can go through this process without difficulty and pain. Now this is not God's Will for us; this is our own will. We are the ones who made guilt, so before we can let it go, we first have to look at it, and this can be very painful. There are two places in particular which describe this process and the amount of terror that is involved: Lessons 170 and 196 (W-pI.170; W-pI.196.9-12). "The Two Worlds" in the text (T-18.IX.3) also talks about the seeming terror that we have to walk through, and the terror of dealing with this fear of God, the final obstacle to peace, which is where our guilt is most deeply buried.

So, the second step really is a willingness to look at our guilt and say that we made it up, and that the guilt represents not God's gift to us, but our decision to see ourselves as God did *not* create us. This is to see oneself as a child of guilt rather than a child of love. *A Course in Miracles* is very clear in emphasizing that because we made guilt, we are not the ones who can undo it. We need help that comes from outside the ego in order to do this. This help is the Holy Spirit. And the one choice that we have is to invite the Holy Spirit to correct the thought system of the ego and have Him take the guilt away from us. This is the third step. The second step, in effect, says to the Holy Spirit: "I no longer want to see myself as guilty; please take it away from me." The third step belongs to the Holy Spirit and He just takes the guilt away because, in effect, He has already taken it away. Our acceptance of this is the only problem.

So to restate the three steps: The first step undoes the projected anger by saying that the problem is not outside me; the problem is inside me. The second step says that the problem that is inside me is one that I made up, and now it is one that I no longer want. The third step occurs, then, when we have handed it over to the Holy Spirit and He takes it from us.

These steps sound very nice and simple, but if you are lucky you will get through it in a lifetime. You should not believe that this will be done overnight. Some people have a magical hope that by getting through the workbook in one year they will be in the Kingdom. Well, that is fine until you get to the very end of the workbook and read: "This course is a beginning, not an end" (W-pII.ep.1:1). The purpose of the workbook is to get us on the right road, to put us in touch with the Holy Spirit, and from then on operate with Him. It is a lifetime's work to undo our guilt because the guilt in us is so enormous, and if we were to confront it all at once we would be overwhelmed, believing we would be struck dead, or would go insane.

80

Therefore, we have to deal with it in chunks at a time. The various experiences and situations that comprise our lives can be used as part of the Holy Spirit's plan to lead us from guilt into guiltlessness.

A Course in Miracles talks a great deal about saving time. In fact, many times it talks about saving thousands of years (e.g., T-1.II.6:7). We are still talking about, in the world's illusion of time, a considerable amount of time. The reason I am emphasizing this is that I do not want you to feel guilty if you still have problems as you keep working with the Course. The real goal on the practical level of the Course is not to be free of problems, but to recognize what they are, and then to recognize within ourselves the means of undoing them.

Again, the purpose of *A Course in Miracles* is very clearly to set forth the ego's thought system and the Holy Spirit's thought system—our wrong-mindedness and right-mindedness—and thus enable us to make the choice against wrong-mindedness and on behalf of forgiveness and the Holy Spirit. This is a slow process and we have to be patient. No one escapes guilt overnight. People who tell you that they transcended their ego probably have not done it. If they truly had, then they would not even tell you because they would be beyond that.

Let me now talk specifically about how this works. And here we see how Jesus and the Holy Spirit would ask us to deal with the situations that come up in our lives. Let us say that I am sitting here as I am trying to be about my Father's business (Lk 2:49), and someone walks in and insults me or throws something at me. Let us assume at the moment while I am sitting here I am not in my right mind. In other words I believe that I am an ego. I feel fearful and guilty, and do not believe that God is with me; I am not really feeling very good about myself. Now you come in and you start ranting and raving at me, accusing me of all kinds of things. At some level because I am guilty I will believe that your attack on me is justified. This has nothing to do with what you say or do not say, or whether what you are saying is true. The fact that I am already guilty will demand that I believe that I should be punished and attacked. You walk in and you do the very thing that I believe I have coming to me. That will do two things. First, your attack on me will reinforce all the guilt that I already feel. Second, it will reinforce the guilt that *you* already feel because you would not be attacking me if you were not already guilty. Your attack on me will reinforce your own guilt.

In this situation I am not going to just sit here and take your attack lying down. I will do one of two things, both of which are the same. One is that I will go into a corner and cry and tell you to look at how terribly you have treated me, to look at how much suffering you have brought upon me, to look at how miserable I feel, and that you should feel responsible for this. The message I would be giving is: because of the terrible thing that you have done to me I am now suffering. This is my way of saying to you that you should feel good and guilty because of what you have done. The other way in which I will do the same thing is to attack you back. I will just call you every name in the book and say: "Where do you come off calling me all these things? *You* are really the evil person, etc."

Both these defenses on my part are really ways of making you feel guilty for what you did to me. The very fact that I am doing that to you constitutes an attack for which I will feel guilty; the very fact that I am imposing guilt on you who are already feeling guilty is going to reinforce your guilt. So what happens at that moment when your guilt meets my guilt is that we reinforce it in each other, and then we are both condemned even more to this prison of guilt in which we live.

This time, let us assume that you come in here and insult me, but now I am in my right mind and I feel good about myself. I know that God is with me, that God loves me and, because of that, nothing can hurt me. No matter what you do to me, because I know that God is with me, I know that I am perfectly safe and secure. I know that no matter what you say, even though it may be true on one level, on a deeper level it cannot be true because I know that I am a Son of God and, therefore, I am perfectly loved by my Father. There is nothing that you can do or say that can take that away from me.

If we assume that this is the position that I am in as I sit here and you come in and insult me, I am then free to look at what you have done in a different way. There is a wonderful line in John's first letter in the New Testament which says, "Perfect love casts out fear" (1 Jn 4:18). Jesus quotes it several times in the Course in different ways (see, for example, T-13.X.10:4; T-20.III.11:3). What that means is not only that perfect love casts out fear, it also casts out sin, guilt, and any form of suffering or anger. There is no way that anyone could be filled with the Love of God (and be identified with it) and be afraid, angry, guilty, or seek to hurt anyone else. It is an absolute impossibility to feel God's Love and to try to hurt another person. You just cannot do it.

This means that if you are trying to hurt me, at that particular moment you do not believe you are filled with God's Love. At that particular moment you are not identifying yourself as a Son of God. You do not believe that God is your Father and, because you are in your ego state, you will feel threatened and guilty. You will feel that God is out to get you. And the only way that you can deal with all of this guilt is to attack a brother of yours. That is what guilt will always do. Therefore your insulting me or your attacking me is really saying: "Please teach me that I am wrong; please teach me that there is a God Who loves me, and that I am His child. Please show me that the love that I believe is impossible for me is really there for me." Therefore, every attack is a call for help or a call for love.

The first section of Chapter 12 of the text, "The Judgment of the Holy Spirit" (T-12.I), is a very clear statement of that. In the eyes of the Holy Spirit every attack is a call for help or a call for love, because if the person felt loved he or she could never attack. The attack is an expression of the fact that the person does not feel loved and, therefore, it is a call for love. It is saying: "Please show me that I am wrong, that there really is a God Who loves me, that I am His child and not the ego's child." If I am sitting here in my right mind, that is what I will hear. I will hear in the attack a call for love. And because at that point I am identified with God's Love, how could I respond in any other way except to try to extend that Love?

The specific form in which I will respond to the attack is up to the Holy Spirit. If I am in my right mind, I will ask Him and He will show me how I should respond. The form in which I act is not important. This is not a course in action or behavior, but one in changing our thinking. As *A Course in Miracles* says, "seek not to change the world, but choose to change your mind about the world" (T-21.in.1:7). If we think in accordance with the Holy Spirit then everything we do will be right. St. Augustine once said, "Love and do what you will." If love is in our heart, everything we do will be right; if it is not in our heart, everything we do will be wrong no matter what it is. Therefore, my concern or interest is not in what I do when you attack me; my interest is in how I can stay in my right mind so I then can ask the Holy Spirit what I should do. Again, if I am in my right mind I will see your attack as being a call for help and not as an attack at all.

This idea of judgment is extremely important. According to the Holy Spirit, again, there are only two judgments that we could ever make about anyone or anything in this world. It is either an expression of love or a call for love. There is no other alternative possible, which makes living in this world very simple once you think like this. If someone is expressing love to me, then how can I respond in any other way except to express love back? If a brother or sister of mine is calling for love, how can I react in any other way than to give that love? Again, it makes living in this world very simple. This means no matter what we do, no matter what the world seems to do to us, our response will always be one of love, which really makes everything very simple. As the Course says, "complexity is of the ego" (T-15.IV.6:2), whereas simplicity is of God. As we follow God's principles, everything we do will always be the same. The section at the end of Chapter 15 was written down at New Year's, and Jesus suggests a New Year's resolution to "make this year different by making it all the same" (T-15.XI.10:11). If you see that everything is either an expression of love or a call for love, then you will always react in the same way: with love.

Forgiveness is my looking beyond the darkness of your attack and seeing it instead as a call for light. That is the vision of Christ, and the goal of *A Course in Miracles* is to help us to meet every situation and person in our lives, without exception, with that vision. To make a single exception is really to say that there is some part of myself that I want to keep shrouded in the darkness of guilt and never have it freed by the light. The way that I will do that is to project it onto you and to see that spot of darkness in you. The final vision of the Course comes on the very last page of the text where it says that "not one spot of darkness still remains to hide the face of Christ from anyone" (T-31.VIII.12:5). Then all the darkness of the guilt in ourselves will be undone. Then we will see the face of Christ which, incidentally, is not the face of Jesus. The face of Christ is the face of innocence that we will see in everyone in the world. At that point we have attained the vision of Christ and that is what the Course refers to as the real world, which is the final goal before Heaven.

What this means in terms of how we live our lives is that we can see every single thing that occurs—from the moment that we are born to the moment that we die, from the moment that we wake each day to the moment that we go to bed each night—as an opportunity that the Holy Spirit can use to help us see ourselves as guiltless. The way that we look upon the people in our lives is the way that we look on ourselves. Therefore, those people who are the most difficult and the most problematic are the greatest gift to us because if we can heal our relationship with them, then what we are really doing is healing our relationship with God.

Every single problem that we see in someone else, that we wish to exclude from our own lives, is really the secret wish to exclude some part of our guilt from ourselves so that we do not have to let it go. That is the ego's attraction of guilt. The best way to hold on to our guilt is to hit someone else over the head. Whenever we are tempted to do that, the Course tells us that there is Someone with us Who will tap us on the shoulder and say: "My brother, choose again" (T-31.VIII.3:2). And the choice is always whether to forgive or not to forgive. The choice we make to forgive someone else is the same choice we make to forgive ourselves. There is no difference between inside and outside; everything is a projection of what we feel inside. If we feel guilt inside, then that is what we will project outside. If we feel the Love of God inside, then that is what we will extend outside. All people and all circumstances in our lives offer us the opportunity of seeing what is inside the projector of our own minds; they offer us the opportunity to make another choice.

Q: I find that the whole idea sounds great, but then I get involved in practical examples of working it out. I can formulate an example where I get in a quandary and cannot see how it can be resolved. For instance, let us say you are working on a project for school. You have an hour to complete it and someone bothers you. At that point you have the choice to act in one way or the other. Suppose the person bothers you again and you still have only an hour to complete the project. At what point can forceful anger be expressed correctly within the right frame of mind?

A: That is a very good question. Henri Nouwen, a professor at Yale, once said that he kept being interrupted in his work until he recognized that the interruptions *were* his work. Someone like myself who always seems to be interrupted should find in this a very helpful lesson. Let me try to give some guidelines.

The issue really depends on how you think you are supposed to spend that hour; whether you believe that it is your goal or that it is God's goal for you. One possibility is that whatever is to be done in that hour really does not need an hour. Maybe it does not have to be done at all. And maybe the person who is interrupting you is more important than the work. Maybe both are important. Maybe the work has to be finished and maybe this person also needs some expression of forgiveness. This is where one's faith is so important. Everything I have said about forgiveness up until now involves what *we* have to do. *A Course in Miracles* makes it very clear that forgiveness cannot be done by ourselves but is done through us by the Holy Spirit. When you seem to be in the position that whatever you do will be wrong, faith would tell you that this does not happen by accident. This is part of some important lessons for you and for the other person.

What you then have to do is go inside of yourself and pray in whatever way you do that and say: "Look, I want to get this project done but here is this person screaming for help. I do not want to see him or her as a pain in the neck, but rather as my brother or sister. Help!" If that really is your goal, to not hurt anyone while getting done what you think you have to get done, somehow it will work out.

That is what a miracle is. A miracle is not anything magical that is happening outside; it is something that happens inside of you that allows this situation to be worked through. That is the principle that you must follow each and every time you have a situation that seems to be insoluble; it is when you are sincere in your motivation that you do not want to hurt anyone, but you do want to do the thing that you are supposed to do, and you do not know how to do it. That is the most honest statement you can make because in and of ourselves we do not know what to do, even when we feel absolutely sure. But there is Someone inside of us Who does know, and He is the One we can go to. That really is the answer to our problem. And that will be the answer to all of our problems.

Let me now talk about "Jesus in the Temple." This is a question that is asked almost every time I talk about anger, especially if it is to a Christian group. You all know the scene of Jesus in the temple. It probably did happen; otherwise it would not have appeared in all four gospels (Mt 21:12; Mk 11:15; Lk 19:45; Jn 2:15). That is one way of finding out if something happened or not, by the way. There are three gospels, Matthew, Mark, and Luke, that constitute one group. And then there is John, which is distinctly different. If something is reported in all four gospels, the chances are that it really did happen. It probably did not always happen as it is written, but the chances are that it happened.

The scene is placed by Matthew, Mark, and Luke at the end of Jesus' life, just before he was arrested. In John, it occurs right at the beginning of his ministry. Jesus is in the temple in Jerusalem, the most sacred place in Judaism. People are charging money for all kinds of things; they are really, in effect, using the temple for their own purposes. And Jesus says to them: "You are treating my Father's house like a den of thieves." In this he is referring to Jeremiah (Jr 7:11). He then overturns the tables where the money-changers are doing their thing and he kicks them out of the temple. Nowhere in the gospel does it ever say that Jesus is angry, by the way, but it describes him as being in a state that could be equivalent to anger. That is the one incident that people use to justify what they call "righteous anger." After all, they say, Jesus got angry so why can't I get angry? An interesting thing about this is that they forgot everything else that is in the gospels where Jesus makes very clear how he feels about anger. You only have to read the Sermon on the Mount where he said: "You have read in the Law where thou shalt not kill. I say unto you that thou shalt not even get angry" (Mt 5:21-22). That is a pretty clear statement, and it describes exactly what he did at the end of his life, when no man seemingly would have been more justified in getting angry than he. But he did not get angry at all.

It is very interesting how people will take one incident and forget everything else. However, I think that there are three basic ways of interpreting that scene. One is that it did not happen the way in which it was written. Now, that can be seen as a cop-out, but there is enough evidence from contemporary scripture scholarship that would indicate that a lot of the angry words that were put into Jesus' mouth were not his at all, but were attributed to him by the early Church which was trying to justify its own position. There is one line where Jesus is quoted as saying, "I come not to bring peace but a sword" (Mt 10:34), which incidentally he reinterprets in the Course (T-6.I.15:2). The *Jerome Biblical Commentary*, which is a very authoritative Catholic scholarly book, asks how the Prince of Peace could ever have said this. It concludes that this was from the early Church and not Jesus himself. So one distinct possibility is that he did not do this in the way that it is described at all.

But setting that aside for a moment, assuming that he did do it that way, the way that I would choose to understand it is this: As any good teacher, Jesus knew how to get his point across in the most effective way possible. This is a very dramatic scene, in full view of all of the people in Jerusalem who are there for Passover, one of three major feasts in Judaism, when everyone was supposed to come to the temple in Jerusalem. This was just before Passover, so the place was filled with people. This was the holiest place on earth for a Jew, and here is where Jesus chose to show very clearly how his Father's temple was to be treated. One way to see this, therefore, is that he was not personally angry, but rather he was trying to make a point in the most dramatic and convincing way possible.

When we speak of anger, there are three major qualities to it. One is that the person who is angry is not at peace. People would not try to maintain that at the moment they are angry they are also peaceful. The two states are mutually exclusive. The second is that at the moment when you are angry, God is the furthest thing from your mind. You are not thinking about God; you are thinking about what that terrible person has done to you. The third quality of anger involves the person with whom you are angry; you are not seeing him or her as your brother or sister at that point at all. Obviously, you see that person as your enemy or else you would not be attacking.

Now I would personally find it difficult to believe that at that stage of Jesus' life anything of this world could have robbed him of his peace, could have caused him to forget about his Father, or caused him to see anyone in the world as not being his brother or sister. So therefore what I think Jesus was doing in the temple was not getting angry as we would get angry, but just making a very forceful presentation and teaching a lesson so that the people would get his point. There are many instances in the gospels where it is very clear that Jesus teaches one way when he teaches the multitudes, quite another way when he teaches his apostles with whom he is most intimate—John, James, or Peter (see, for example, Mt 5; Mk 9:2). There are levels of teaching as any teacher knows. The temple was a public place where he was trying to get people's attention to make his point. He therefore was not personally angry at the people he was casting out.

There is still a third way of explaining all this which is to say that Jesus had an ego attack. He just got fed up, became impatient and angry, and ranted and raved. I personally cannot believe that this could be so at that point in his life. But if you do say that that is what he did, the question would still be why you want to identify with his ego instead of the Christ in him, and all of the other things that he taught, said, and exemplified.

So the three explanations are: (1) it did not happen like that at all, (2) he was just trying to teach at a different level and was not angry, or (3) he just had an ego attack, and why would you want to identify with that when there are much better ways of handling that problem?

Q: Why is it that anger is used so much in psychotherapy as therapeutic, working it out and that sort of thing?

A: Most psychotherapy is of the ego. It is unfortunate that the psychology of the past twenty or thirty years has discovered anger and has made it into an idol.

Let me talk a little about anger, which is one of the great problems in the world. The pamphlet *Psychotherapy: Purpose, Process and Practice*[*] speaks about the problem of psychotherapy as really that of anger. The reason for that is that anger is the prominent defense against guilt. Anger keeps us riveted outside of ourselves.

It is interesting to think of anger in terms of its history throughout this century, especially as psychologists have seen it. That provides the background for

---

[*] *Psychotherapy: Purpose, Process and Practice* (Mill Valley, CA: Foundation for Inner Peace, 1976).

how people are seeing it now. For about the first fifty years of this century, psychology was dominated by Freud and psychoanalysis. It is always helpful when we read Freud and see the influence that he had, to recall that he did all of his work in a very Victorian atmosphere. Vienna at the turn of the century was very much influenced by Victorian values, and Freud was really just a child of his time. This meant that he had a distinct bias and was afraid of feelings, and consequently the expression of them. The interesting thing is that his whole theory is intended to free us from repression, yet the attitude that he held personally and conveyed in his theories is that we should not express feelings. We can analyze, sublimate, or displace them, but we should not express them. We will concentrate here on the one feeling of anger.

The dominant feeling in psychology and psychotherapy was that you taught people to analyze their feelings or to sublimate them, or displace them onto other things. However, they were not to express them. Certainly this was a predominant Christian value as well. A "real" Christian turns the other cheek, which means that we get slammed in the face twice, as the teaching was taught and understood. (That is not the way that Jesus meant it, incidentally—that we be victims who suffer in his name.) All of this got reinforced in the idea that anger was something to be feared. It was considered a bad thing that should be pushed down and repressed. After the Second World War there was a revolution in psychology. Suddenly people discovered that they had feelings. What emerged was the whole movement of T-groups, sensitivity groups, sensitivity training, encounter groups, marathon groups, etc. People therefore became very good at breaking through the defenses against anger and experiencing all of their feelings and emotions, especially anger.

The pendulum swung from one extreme to the other. Instead of people being taught to repress anger and to analyze it, the criterion for mental health now became getting the feelings out. And people have become very good at expressing their feelings. Thus, two basic alternatives were established, one to repress anger and the other to express it. If we continuously repress our anger, we are going to get ulcers and gastrointestinal problems. On the other hand, if we always express our anger we will be doing exactly what I spoke of earlier: we will only be reinforcing the very guilt that underlies the anger. So there seems to be no way out.

The key to understanding the problem is to see the premise that underlies both of these alternatives, and the interesting thing is that it is the same premise. The solutions seem to be entirely different—one is repression and one is expression—yet the premise is the same. It is really heads and tails of the same coin. The premise is that anger is a basic human emotion that is inherent in the human species. Therefore, when anger is discussed, it is described almost as if it were a quantifiable mass of energy. There is something inherent in us that makes us human that includes anger, and we have to do something with it. If we push it down and keep it inside, then it erupts inside of us and we get ulcers. Alternatively, we can get this mass of energy outside of us and out of our system, and then it seems to feel so good to get this terrible burden of anger out. The real reason that an expression of anger feels so good has nothing to do with getting the anger out. Instead, what seems to occur is that for the first time we believe that we have finally gotten rid of this burden of guilt.

The basic human emotion then is not anger; it is guilt. This is the fallacy that underlies the whole approach that the world takes in looking at anger. *A Course in Miracles* has a lovely section called "The Two Emotions" (T-13.V) in which it says that we have only two emotions. One was given to us and the other we made. The one that was given to us is love; this was given by God. And the one that we made as a substitute for love is fear. Once again, we can always substitute guilt for fear.

The basic human emotion, which is the basic ego emotion, is fear or guilt. It is not anger. Anger is a projection of guilt and is never the problem. The real problem is always the underlying guilt. The reason that we feel so good when we vent our anger at someone is that in that instant we believe that we have finally gotten rid of our guilt. The problem comes the next morning or several mornings later when we wake up and we feel rotten. We then experience the psychological hangover that is known as depression. We do not know where the depression is coming from. We blame it on all kinds of things. We do not realize that the real reason for our depression is that we feel guilty for what we did to this other person. Whenever we get angry or attack, we will later feel guilty. People speak of depression as unexpressed rage. On one level this is true, but underneath the rage is guilt. The real meaning of depression is guilt or self-hatred.

Now that I have told you all of these terrible things about anger let me say that there is one circumstance where an expression of anger can be positive, and this is what the question was about. This involves looking at anger from a therapeutic point of view. If we have been taught all of our lives that anger is bad, as is probably true for everyone in this room, then what we have really been taught is that anger is fearful. We believe that if we express anger, something terrible will happen to the other person; or even worse, something terrible will happen to us. It can then be therapeutically very helpful, as part of the process of being freed entirely from the anger and guilt, to go through a period of time when we do express anger and experience that it is no big deal. We can get angry at people and they will not drop dead at our feet. We can get angry at someone and God will not strike us dead because of the terrible thing that we have done. In effect nothing terrible will happen at all. It is no big deal. At that point we can look at the anger more objectively and recognize that the problem is not anger at all. The real problem is the anger we are directing at ourselves for our guilt.

The danger is that we will not see this as a temporary step. Thanks to the recent teachings of psychology, we will see this as an end. What happens then is that anger is worshipped as an idol because it feels so good to haul off and get angry at another person. Psychology will never teach us (because psychology is really a very secular system) that the real problem is guilt, and that the guilt is a defense against God. What happens then is that the expression of anger becomes the goal, and it feels so good that we do not want to let it go. However, our goal really should be to get in touch with and deal with the underlying guilt. We need to express our anger only as a phase in getting beyond it entirely. So if we go through a period when we feel a need to get angry, we should see it as a temporary stage and try to see the anger as no big deal. Then we can get to the real problem, which is guilt. When we actually deal with the guilt and let it go, we will never need to get angry again.

Q: One point that I have gotten from listening to Mr. Krishnamurti is his suggestion of the possibility that the change can be immediate.

A: *A Course in Miracles* says the same thing. It says that this whole thing could end in an instant. But then there are other places where it says that this will take a long time and you have to be patient. Right at the beginning of the text is a line that I am sure has upset many, many people. It talks about the Last Judgment, which is really the collective undoing of the ego or the completion of the Atonement. It says that "just as the separation occurred over millions of years, the Last Judgment will extend over a similarly long period, and perhaps an even longer one" (T-2.VIII. 2:5). It does say right after that, however, that the time can be considerably shortened by miracles. But it is really not likely to happen overnight. If you just think about how our world is constituted, there is a tremendous amount of fear that underlies and motivates every single aspect of it. Every institution, every system of thought within this world is motivated by fear and guilt. You just cannot change that right now. I think the plan of the Atonement and the Course's part in it is to change individuals' minds much more quickly than would otherwise happen. That is what the "celestial speed-up"* is, but it is still happening within a framework of a considerable period of time.

The Meaning of Miracles

I should say something about miracles, since that *is* the name of the book. That is another of the words that is used differently. *A Course in Miracles* uses the word "miracle" simply to mean a correction, the undoing of a false perception. It is a shift in perception, it is forgiveness, it is the means of healing. All of those words are basically the same. It has nothing to do with anything external. A so-called miracle in terms of something external, such as walking on water or an external healing, is just a reflection of the internal miracle. A miracle is an inner shift. One of the loveliest lines in the Course defines a miracle this way: "The holiest of all the spots on earth is where an ancient hatred has become a present love" (T-26.IX.6:1). That is a miracle. When you suddenly shift from a perception of hatred

---

* See footnote, p. 22.

for someone to where you look with love on that person, that is a miracle. It is a shift in perception; it is a correction of the ego's way of looking to the Holy Spirit's way of looking.

That is why it is a course in miracles; it tells us how to do this. It talks about how to change our minds. Again, we do not change the world, we change our minds about the world. We do not seek to change another person; we change how we are looking at that person. The Holy Spirit will then work through us to do whatever He thinks is best. It is a change in mind with a shift in perception. That is what a miracle is, and that is the goal of the Course.

Now let me talk a little bit about the role of God and the Holy Spirit in this. One of the important qualities of *A Course in Miracles* is that it is a religious book. It is not just a self-help book, or a sound psychological system which, of course, it is too. It is also a deeply religious book. Its religious aspects are centered on two points of view. The first is that without God we have nothing left but the ego. Unless we know that there is a God Who created us, Whose Son we are, we are stuck with whatever image or perception we have about ourselves which will always be some offshoot of the ego. True forgiveness is impossible unless it is first nourished in the belief that we are invulnerable. In other words, we cannot be harmed by anyone or anything in the world; such a belief is impossible unless we know that there is a God Who created us and Who loves us. So this is the foundation for the whole thought system that the Holy Spirit is offering us, as expressed by the Course.

The second part of the importance of God in all this is a little more practical. True forgiveness is impossible without the Holy Spirit. This is true from two points of view. First, we are not the ones who forgive; we are not the ones who undo guilt. Strictly speaking, when *A Course in Miracles* speaks of forgiveness, it is really speaking of the decision we make to let the Holy Spirit's forgiveness come through us. In and of ourselves we can never forgive, because in and of ourselves, at least in this world, we are the ego. We cannot change a thought system from within the thought system. We need help from outside the thought system—help that enters into the thought system and then transforms it. That help from outside of the ego's thought system is the Holy Spirit. So He is the One Who forgives through us.

The second thing is even more important and will answer a number of questions that people have raised. Forgiveness is the most difficult thing in the world, which is why hardly anyone does it and why the whole concept of forgiveness that Jesus gave was so bitterly misunderstood from the time he gave it. The reason is that when we truly forgive, as the Course speaks of it, we are really letting go of our own guilt. And no one who identifies with the ego wants to do this. Without God's help there is no way that we can get through some of the deeper problems of guilt that will confront us.

If you think of time as a continuum, a carpet is a very helpful image to use in describing this whole process.

The Carpet of Time

GOD CHRIST	real world	ego - guilt ⟶
		world - body - form - time
		⟵ Holy Spirit - forgiveness

When the separation occurred, this whole carpet of time spun out, and ever since, we have walked the carpet away from God. The further we went away from God, the deeper we got involved with the world and the problems of guilt and sin. When we ask the Holy Spirit to help us, we reverse this process and begin to walk towards God. Several of the most interesting sections of the Course talk about time. These are very hard to understand because we are still stuck in it. At one point it says that time seems to go forward, but it is really going backward to the point at which time began (T-2.II.6; M-2.3; 4:1-2). This is when the separation occurred. The whole purpose of the Atonement is the Holy Spirit's plan to undo the ego. And it is rolled up in this carpet of time. The ego would have us unroll it more and more, whereas the Holy Spirit would have us roll it back up to the beginning.

As we roll it back, which forgiveness and the miracle do, we get closer to the very bedrock of the ego system. The very beginning of the carpet is the birth of the ego, which is the home of sin and guilt. And this is the deepest part of the ego system. If you think of the image of the iceberg that I mentioned earlier, the very bottom of the iceberg is the hard-core guilt that we all feel.

As we get closer to the guilt and the fear that we have spent a lifetime (if not many lifetimes) running away from, we will really be thrown into a panic. This guilt is the most devastating and frightening thing in the world. That is why the process is a slow one and why we must be patient as we pursue it. If we go too quickly, we will not be prepared for the onslaught of guilt that will hit us. In the last two paragraphs of the first chapter of the text (T-1.VII.4-5), we read of the need to go very slowly and carefully through all of the material, including the first four chapters. If we do not, we will not be prepared for what will come later, and we will become afraid of it. That is when people throw the book away.

We have to work slowly through all of this material in ourselves, not to mention the Course itself, because otherwise our fear will get aroused to an extent greater than we can handle. So as we get closer to the bedrock of the ego system, we will become more afraid of the guilt that is buried there. Unless we know that there is Someone walking with us Who is holding our hand, Who is not ourself and Who loves us, we will not be able to take that step.

A Course in Miracles teaches that the goal of this process of undoing our guilt is not to awaken from the dream entirely, but to live in the "real world" or the "happy dream." Thus, as the carpet gets rolled back, we eventually reach a state of mind in which we no longer have any guilt to project, and therefore are at peace all the time, regardless of what is going on in the external world. This state of mind is the "real world," and is a concept which reflects the gentleness of the Course's path. As the text says, "God willed he waken gently and with joy, and gave him means to waken without fear" (T-27.VII.13:5).

One of the things that I am frequently asked is how I talk about forgiveness to people who do not believe in God. I had occasion just this week to address senior citizens at a home where my mother does volunteer work. This is a Jewish organization, but most of the people are really not religious as we would think of it. I spoke about forgiveness, which is what I always speak of. It was an interesting challenge. I tried not to bring God too much into it, as that would have alienated the people even more. But it is very difficult to talk about forgiveness without bringing God into it, because without God true forgiveness cannot be done.

The early stages of the process of forgiveness can be done by everyone, because we can always be taught to see people differently. But as we get into some of the really difficult problems in our lives, and ultimately these will be problems of forgiveness, we must know that there is Someone with us Who loves us. Yet that Person is not ourselves. That Person is the Holy Spirit, or Jesus, or whatever name we choose to give Him. Without His help we will be too frightened to go the rest of the way; we will be willing to go only so far. So the Holy Spirit is not only our Guide and our Teacher, He also is our Comforter. At the very end of the workbook Jesus says: "and of this be sure; that I will never leave you comfortless" (W-pII.ep.6:8). Unless we know that he means those words very literally, that there is Someone in us Who is not of us, Who will love and comfort us, we will never be able to get past that bedrock of the ego system when we have to deal with our own guilt. Again, this is always done in the context of forgiving another person. Neither Jesus nor the Holy Spirit cares what name we choose for Them. But They do care that we recognize that there is Someone with us from God, Who is taking our hand

and leading us through. Without that feeling of comfort and assurance, we will never be able to get past the ego. And again, this is why when things seem to be getting worse, they might truly be getting better.

There are two sections in Chapter 9 in the text that are very helpful: "The Two Evaluations" (T-9.VII) and "Grandeur versus Grandiosity" (T-9.VIII). These are two clear statements of how the ego will attack us and get vicious just when we are following the Holy Spirit. Remember that to the ego the guiltless are guilty. When we betray the ego and begin to choose guiltlessness instead of guilt, the ego will let us know it in spades. That is why the Course says that the ego's emotions range from suspiciousness to viciousness (T-9.VII.4:7). When we really start to take the Holy Spirit seriously, the ego will get downright vicious. This is when things will seem to get difficult.

I am now talking about this as an abstract principle, but as we go through it, it is anything but abstract. It can be the most devastating, powerful, and painful thing we will ever experience. Once again, unless we know that there is Someone with us Who speaks for truth and love, and Who sees us differently, we will never get through it. We will just throw the book away, hide under the bed, and never come out. Or we will run the other way. This is why the process has to be done slowly and why we are carefully led along. The plan of the Atonement for each of us is very carefully devised, which explains the varying times it takes us to complete it.

A Course in Miracles explains that the Atonement curriculum is individualized (M-29.2:6), which means that the Holy Spirit corrects for us all the specific forms in which we as individuals have manifested our shared error of separation. We are not the ones who make the plan of this curriculum. We do not even understand what the plan is in truth. And we definitely do not take ourselves through it. It is therefore important that we not confuse ourselves with God, for if we do there is no one we can turn to when the going gets rough.

While it is true that the Course says that the Holy Spirit will always "send" people in the world to help us, the ultimate purpose of these people is to lead us to know that the Person Who can help the most is inside. Thank God that there are people who can hold our hand as we go through things. However, the ultimate Source of comfort will always be from within, for that is where God has placed the Answer. Again I must stress that this is a slow process. If we go too quickly, the fear will become overwhelming before we have developed sufficient confidence in ourself or in God. The confidence in ourself is really in knowing that the Holy Spirit is there to help us through it. As we progress and practice all of our daily lessons, we begin to recognize that all of the miracles and changes that are occurring are not being done by us. They are done *through* us but not *by* us. There is Someone Who is helping us go through it.

One of the things that *A Course in Miracles* makes very clear is the importance of developing a personal relationship with either Jesus or the Holy Spirit. From the perspective of function, it makes no difference whom you choose. They both function as our internal Teachers, and the Course alternates in using Them in this way. When the Course stresses the need for this personal relationship with our internal Teacher, it does not speak of the Holy Spirit as an abstract Being. It speaks of Him as a Person and uses the pronoun "He." It also speaks often of Him as an expression of God's Love for us. This is also true when Jesus is speaking of his own role. The Course therefore wants us to develop a sense that there is Someone inside of us, not an abstract force, but a real Person Who loves us and will help us. If we do not have this feeling of assurance we will stop far short of the goal because the fear will just become too overwhelming. If you do not yet have this personal experience of the Holy Spirit, you should not panic. Just be patient and He will show up on His own. It is enough for you to know that there is Someone helping you, whether you feel it or just know intellectually. He will make Himself known to you in whatever form you can accept. The form is not important. What is important, however, is the awareness that there is Someone with you Who is not of you. He is in you but not of you, coming from a part of you that is not your ego self.

Q: We have free choice. Couldn't we choose to have the time accelerated if we feel ready?

A: Yes, absolutely. That is what a miracle does.

Q: That would be in terms of a lifetime, so why must we think in terms of millions of years?

A: Millions of years refers to the whole Sonship. The Last Judgment would be the end of the material universe as we know it. However, one individual can shorten the time considerably.

So once again, if we are going along fine and something really starts hammering at our head, it is probably a good sign. It indicates that the ego has gotten frightened. The ego then will try to make us doubt the Voice that we have been hearing. It will try to make us doubt the Course, and try to make us doubt everything that we have been learning that has been working for us. Therefore we should expect it, but not try to bring it about. But when the ego attack does occur we will know what it is, and it is very helpful to be able to recognize the ego for what it is. Again, the ego attack comes just when we think we are becoming egoless, so keep this in mind when the going gets rough. It does not at all mean that the whole thing is a sham. It means that we have gotten frightened, which means that our ego has become afraid. At that point we should step back, take the hand of Jesus, and ask for his help in looking at our fear. The very fact that we are taking his hand shows that we are not our ego. Then we will look at the ego attack and realize that it is not what it seems to be.

There is an important section called "Above the Battleground" (T-23.IV) in which Jesus asks us to raise ourselves above the battlefield and look down on what is happening. From this perspective we will see things differently. But if we stay in the middle of it, all we will see is a lot of pain, killing, and guilt. If we can raise our viewpoint to look down on the ego's battlefield, then we will see it differently. We will see that it is only our ego jumping up and down. And we will see that this really does not make any difference. This process does take time. We should not expect it to happen overnight. But when it does happen at least we will recognize that it is only our ego giving us a hard time. This is not reality. Reality is that there is a God Who loves us, and that He has sent Someone to represent Him, either Jesus or the Holy Spirit, Who is holding our hand and leading us through the difficult time.

Q: Can this be what happens when I meditate? Is that what is happening when I go through stages when I just cannot possibly face myself during meditation, and there is a lot of chatter? Is that the ego fighting?

A: Yes. What you must do is recognize this and not take it too seriously. Do not fight against it. When you fight against it, you are making the problem real. So what you want to do is step back, look at it, and laugh. There are several places in the Course where it tells us that we should laugh at the ego. In one place, it says that this dream that we think is the world is a dream which began when the Son of God forgot to laugh (T-27.VIII.6:2-3). If we can laugh at the world and at the ego it will disappear as a problem. The worst thing we can do is to fight against the problem, as that makes it seem real. However, this laughter is certainly not derisive, nor should it be thought of as encouraging indifference to people's specific expressions of the basic problem of separation.

Chapter 5

JESUS: THE PURPOSE OF HIS LIFE

The reason that I think it is important now to talk about Jesus is that everyone seems to have trouble with him, for some of the reasons that I spoke of earlier. Growing up in the world, whether it be as a Christian or a Jew, a person's notion of Jesus will be a distorted one. In *A Course in Miracles*, he wants to set the record straight. He wants people to see him as a loving brother, rather than a brother of judgment, death, guilt, and suffering, or a non-existent brother. That is why the Course came as it did and why Jesus makes such a point of being the author of it. Let me speak first about how Jesus describes himself and the purpose of his life.

One of the most important concepts in *A Course in Miracles* is that of cause and effect. It is a helpful way of looking at the whole idea of forgiveness, especially in looking at the mission of Jesus and how he fulfilled it. The very nature of cause and effect is such that we cannot have one without the other. What establishes something as a cause is that it leads to an effect. And what establishes something as an effect is that it has come from a cause.

One of my favorite lines in the Course seems almost incomprehensible. It says: "The cause a cause is *made* by its effects" (T-28.II.1:2). This is a poetic way of saying that a cause is made a cause by its effects. So what establishes something as a cause is that it has an effect. Likewise, what establishes something as an effect is that it has a cause. This is a fundamental principle of this world and also of Heaven. God is the First Cause, and the Effect is His Son. So God is the Cause that established His Son as the Effect. And as an Effect of God, we therefore establish God as being the Creator or the Father.

The principle also works in this world, such that every action will have a reaction. What this also means is that if something is not a cause it cannot exist in this world. Everything in this world must have an effect; otherwise it would not exist. Every action must have a reaction: That is a fundamental principle of physics. If something exists, it will have an effect on something else. Therefore everything that exists in this world will be a cause and will have an effect, and it is this effect that establishes the cause. Okay? Getting this principle is very important because then we can use it as an abstract formula and plug into it.

Think back to the biblical story of original sin. When God caught up with Adam and Eve and punished them, He expressed the punishment within a causal context. He said: "Because of what you have done, this is what will happen. Because you have sinned, the effect of your sin will be a life of suffering." Sin therefore is the cause of all the suffering of this world. The sin of separation, which gave birth to the ego, gives rise to its effect: a life of suffering, pain, and eventually death.

Everything that we know in this world is the effect of our belief in sin. Sin therefore is the cause, of which pain, suffering, and death are the effect. St. Paul made a brilliant statement when he said: "For the wages of sin *is* death" (Rm 6:23). (This is also quoted in the Course [T-19.II.3:6].) He was saying exactly the same thing. Sin is the cause, and death is the effect. There is no more powerful witness to the reality of the separated world than death. That is a prominent theme of the Course.

So death then becomes the ultimate proof that sin is real. Death is the effect of sin, which is the cause. If we now attempt to follow the Holy Spirit's thinking and we want to prove that this world is not real and that the sin of separation never happened, all that is needed is to prove that sin has no effect. If we could prove that the cause had no effect, then the cause can no longer exist. If something is not a cause it is not real. Everything that is real must be a cause and thus have an effect. If we remove the effect we are also eliminating the cause.

Now, if the greatest effect of sin in this world is death, demonstrating that death is an illusion simultaneously demonstrates that there is no sin. This also says that the separation never occurred. We therefore need someone to show us that there is no death. By undoing death, that person will also undo sin and will simultaneously show us that there is no separation, that the separation never occurred, and the only reality, the only true Cause, is God. That person was Jesus. And his mission was to show that there is no death.

The principle of cause and effect is summarized in the following diagram:

	CAUSE ◄——————► EFFECT	
Heaven	God (Father) ◄——————►	Christ (Son)
world	sin ◄——————►	suffering sickness death

The gospels speak of Jesus as the lamb of God who takes away the sins of the world (e.g., Jn 1:29). The way that he took away the sins of the world was to show that they had no effect. Through his overcoming of death, he took away all sins. However, this is not the way the Churches have understood it, or that it has been taught. So one important reason that the Course has come at this time, in this way, is to correct this error. What Jesus did was to live in this world—the world of suffering, sin, and death—and show that it had no effect on him.

The entire basis of *A Course in Miracles* rests on the understanding that the resurrection of Jesus actually occurred. Strictly speaking, the resurrection is only the awakening from the dream of death. It is thus concerned only with the mind and not the body. But keeping to its usage of traditional Christian language, the Course frequently uses the term "resurrection" to correspond to the traditional understanding. Jesus said: "Teach not that I died in vain. Teach rather that I did not die by demonstrating that I live in you" (T-11.VI.7:3-4). He says the same thing many times in different ways. The crucial thing to understand, then, is that there is no death, because if death is real, then every other form of suffering is real, and God is dead. Furthermore, if sin is real, it means that a part of God has separated itself from God, which means that there cannot be a God. God and His Son cannot be separated.

So Jesus took on the most compelling witness to the reality of this world and he showed that it had no hold over him. That was the whole meaning of his life, his mission, and his function. To overcome death is to show that death is not real, that its seeming cause also is not real, and that we therefore never really separated ourselves from our Father. This is the undoing of the separation. The Course speaks of the Holy Spirit as being the principle of the Atonement. The moment that the separation seemed to occur, God placed the Holy Spirit in us, which undid the separation. That is the principle, but the principle had to become manifest in this world. And Jesus was the one who manifested the principle of the Atonement through his own life, death, and resurrection.

Once again, to benefit from *A Course in Miracles*, it is not necessary to believe in Jesus as our personal savior, Lord, or whatever other words we choose to use. But on some level we must accept the fact that the resurrection is something that could have happened, even though we may not believe in Jesus. Ultimately, we cannot accept the Course unless we also accept the fact that death is an illusion. We need not do this right away, and we do not have to fully integrate this into our lives, because the moment that we fully integrate it, we will not be here any more. This is the goal. But as an intellectual idea, we have to recognize it as an essential part of the entire system.

Q: When you say that we will not be here anymore, do you mean that we will die?

A: Well, it actually means that we *need* not be here for our own Atonement; eventually we will have served the purpose of our being here. When that purpose is served, we can then lay down our body and be back Home. That is a nice thought, not a bad thought as we generally see it.

This principle of cause and effect also operates in terms of forgiveness, and Jesus offers some of the best demonstrations of this. Think back once again to the example of me sitting here when someone comes in and attacks me. If I am not in my right mind, I will see that person as the cause of my suffering. My suffering then will be the effect of that person's sin. My reaction of being hurt will reinforce the fact that this person has sinned. If I am in my right mind, I will turn the other cheek, which means in this sense, that I will show that person that his or her sin against me had no effect because I have not been hurt. By cancelling the effect, I am also cancelling the cause. That is true forgiveness.

Jesus showed us this example, not only through his resurrection, but in various actions at the end of his life. This is presented in a very powerful section in the text called "The Message of the Crucifixion" (T-6.I).

People were attacking, humiliating, mocking, and insulting him, and they finally killed him. In sinning against him, they appeared to be causing him to suffer. The fact that he did not attack them back but continued to love and forgive them, was his way of saying that their sin against him was without effect; therefore they had not sinned. They had merely been mistaken. They had merely called out for help. And that is how Jesus forgave us our sins, not only during his life, but then surely in his resurrection. His resurrection clearly said that the world's sin of murder against him was without effect. He is still with us; therefore they could not have killed him, which means that they did not sin. They had only looked at their "sin" wrongly. That is the Holy Spirit's plan of forgiveness that the Course describes. You undo the cause by showing that it had no effect.

The most difficult thing in all the world is to meet attack with forgiveness. Yet that is the only thing that God asks of us. That is also the only thing that Jesus asks of us. And the beautiful thing is that not only did he give us this perfect example of how this should be done, but he also has remained within us to help us do the same thing. No one could meet the attacks of the world without knowing that there is someone within us who is protecting, loving, and comforting us, and asking us to share his love with the person who is attacking us. We cannot do this without his help. And that is the plea that Jesus makes over and over again in *A Course in Miracles*—that we accept his help to forgive.

Q: So does this mean that when we truly forgive another after being attacked, it is not our ego forgiving, but that we have "become" the manifestation of the Holy Spirit and it is He who forgives?

A: Yes. When Jesus says in the Course that he is the manifestation of the Holy Spirit, he means that he does not have any other voice. The Holy Spirit is described as the Voice for God. God does not have two voices. Jesus no longer has an ego, so the only other Voice that is available to him is that of the Holy Spirit, and he is the manifestation of It. To the extent that we can identify with him, and join with him in sharing his perception of the world (the vision of Christ), we also become manifestations of the Holy Spirit, and our voice will become His Voice. Then every time we open our mouths to speak, it would be His Voice that is heard. And that really is what Jesus asks of us.

One of the most beautiful lines in the Course is in the introduction to the fifth review in the workbook (W-pI.rV.9:2-3). This is one of the few places in the workbook where Jesus speaks about himself. Paraphrased, the passage reads: "I need your eyes, your hands, and your feet. I need your voice through which

I save the world." This means that without us he cannot save the world. That is what he means in the text when he says: "I need you as much as you need me" (T-8.V.6:10). His voice cannot be heard in the world unless it comes through us, because no one can listen to it otherwise. It has to come through specific forms and bodies in this world for other bodies to hear it. Otherwise, he will always remain a symbolic abstraction that means very little. He needs us to let go of our ego enough to allow him to speak through us. There is a lovely prayer of Cardinal Newman that ends with: "And as they look up let them not see me, but only Jesus." When people hear us speak, let them not hear us, but only his words.

It is not necessary to personally identify with Jesus as an historical person, someone who was crucified and "arose from the dead." It is not even necessary to identify with him as the author of the Course or as our teacher. It is necessary, however, to forgive him. If we do not, we are holding something against him that we are really holding against ourselves. He does not ask that we take him as our personal teacher. He only asks that we look at him differently and not make him responsible for what other people have made of him. At one point in the Course the Holy Spirit says: "Some bitter idols have been made of him who would be only brother to the world" (C-5.5:7). Just as Freud said, "I am not a Freudian," Jesus could say, "I am not a

Christian." Nietzsche said that the last Christian died on the cross, which unfortunately is probably true.

In summary, then, we can recall Jesus' words in *A Course in Miracles*, that we take him as our model for learning (T-5.II.9:6-7; 12:1-3; T-6.in.2:1; T-6.I.7:2; 8:6-7). This certainly does not mean that we need to be crucified as he was, but rather that we identify with the meaning of his death; namely, when we find ourselves tempted to feel that we are unfairly treated, the innocent victims of what the world has done to us, we should recall Jesus' example and ask his help. In the eyes of the world, he was unquestionably an innocent victim, and yet that was not a perception he shared. He asks us therefore, usually under far less extreme conditions than in his life, to remember that we can only be victimized by our thoughts, and that the peace and Love of God that is our true Identity can never be affected by what others do or even seem to do to us. That remembrance is the basis of forgiveness, and our learning it is the purpose of *A Course in Miracles*.

INDEX OF REFERENCES TO *A COURSE IN MIRACLES*

text

text (cont.)

workbook for students

workbook for students (cont.)

manual for teachers

clarification of terms

Foundation for A COURSE IN MIRACLES®

Kenneth Wapnick *received his Ph.D. in Clinical Psychology in 1968 from Adelphi University. He was a close friend and associate of Helen Schucman and William Thetford, the two people whose joining together was the immediate stimulus for the scribing of A COURSE IN MIRACLES. Kenneth has been involved with A COURSE IN MIRACLES since 1973, writing, teaching, and integrating its principles with his practice of psychotherapy. He is on the Executive Board of the Foundation for Inner Peace, publishers of A COURSE IN MIRACLES.*

In 1983, with his wife Gloria, he began the Foundation for A COURSE IN MIRACLES, and in 1984 this evolved into a Teaching and Healing Center in Crompond, New York, which was quickly outgrown. In 1988 they opened the Academy and Retreat Center in upstate New York. In 1995 they began the Institute for Teaching Inner Peace through A COURSE IN MIRACLES, an educational corporation chartered by the New York State Board of Regents. In 2001 the Foundation moved to Temecula, California, and shifted its emphasis to electronic teaching. The Foundation publishes a quarterly newsletter, "The Lighthouse," which is available free of charge. The following is Kenneth's and Gloria's vision of the Foundation.

In our early years of studying *A Course in Miracles,* as well as teaching and applying its principles in our respective professions of psychotherapy, and teaching and school administration, it seemed evident that this was not the simplest of thought systems to understand. This was so not only in the intellectual grasp of its teachings, but perhaps more importantly in the application of these teachings to our personal lives. Thus, it appeared to us from the beginning that the Course lent itself to teaching, parallel to the ongoing teachings of the Holy Spirit in the daily opportunities within our relationships, which are discussed in the early pages of the manual for teachers.

One day several years ago while Helen Schucman and I (Kenneth) were discussing these ideas, she shared a vision that she had had of a teaching center as a white temple with a gold cross atop it. Although it was clear that this image was symbolic, we understood it to be representative of what the teaching center was to be: a place where the person of Jesus and his message in *A Course in Miracles* would be manifest. We have sometimes seen an image of a lighthouse shining its light into the sea, calling to it those passers-by who sought it. For us, this light is the Course's teaching of forgiveness, which we would hope to share with those who are drawn to the Foundation's form of teaching and its vision of *A Course in Miracles*.

This vision entails the belief that Jesus gave the Course at this particular time in this particular form for several reasons. These include:

1) the necessity of healing the mind of its belief that attack is salvation; this is accomplished through forgiveness, the undoing of our belief in the reality of separation and guilt.

2) emphasizing the importance of Jesus and/or the Holy Spirit as our loving and gentle Teacher, and developing a personal relationship with this Teacher.

3) correcting the errors of Christianity, particularly where it has emphasized suffering, sacrifice, separation, and sacrament as being inherent in God's plan for salvation.

Our thinking has always been inspired by Plato (and his mentor Socrates), both the man and his teachings. Plato's Academy was a place where serious and thoughtful people came to study his philosophy in an atmosphere conducive to their learning, and then returned to their professions to implement what they were taught by the great philosopher. Thus, by integrating abstract philosophical ideals with experience, Plato's school seemed to be the perfect model for the teaching center that we directed for so many years.

We therefore see the Foundation's principal purpose as being to help students of *A Course in Miracles* deepen their understanding of its thought system, conceptually and experientially, so that they may be more effective instruments of Jesus' teaching in their own lives. Since teaching forgiveness without experiencing it is empty, one of the Foundation's specific goals is to help facilitate the process whereby people may be better able to know that their own sins are forgiven and that they are truly loved by God. Thus is the Holy Spirit able to extend His Love through them to others.

Responding in part to the "electronic revolution," we have taken the Foundation's next step in our move to Temecula, California. With this move to a non-residential setting we are shifting our focus, though not exclusively, from totally live presentations to electronic and digital forms of teaching in order to maximize the benefits of the burgeoning field of electronic media communication. This will allow us to increase our teaching outreach, the *content* of which will remain the same, allowing its *form* to adapt to the 21st century.

Related Material on
A Course in Miracles

By Kenneth Wapnick, Ph.D.

Books
(For a complete list and full descriptions of our books and audio and video publications, please see our Web site at www.facim.org, or call or write for our free catalog.)

Christian Psychology in *A Course in Miracles*. Second edition, enlarged.
ISBN 978-0-933291-14-0 • #B-1 • Paperback • 90 pages • $5.

    Translation available in Spanish.

Glossary-Index for *A Course in Miracles*. Fifth edition, revised and enlarged.
ISBN 978-0-933291-03-4 • #B-4 • Paperback • 349 pages • $10.

    Translations available in Spanish and *German.*

Forgiveness and Jesus: The Meeting Place of *A Course in Miracles* and Christianity. Sixth edition.
ISBN 978-0-933291-13-3 • #B-5 • Paperback • 399 pages • $16.

    Translations available in Spanish and German.

The Fifty Miracle Principles of *A Course in Miracles*. Fifth edition.
ISBN 978-0-933291-15-7 • #B-6 • Paperback • 107 pages • $8.

    Translations available in Spanish and German.

Awaken from the Dream. Second edition. Gloria and Kenneth Wapnick.
ISBN 978-0-933291-04-1 • #B-7 • Paperback • 132 pages • $10.

    Translations available in German and Spanish.

Love Does Not Condemn: The World, the Flesh, and the Devil According to Platonism, Christianity, Gnosticism, and *A Course in Miracles*.
ISBN 978-0-933291-07-2 • #B-9 • Hardcover • 614 pages • $25.

A Vast Illusion: Time According to *A Course in Miracles*. Second edition.
ISBN 978-0-933291-09-6 • #B-10 • Paperback • 310 pages • $14.

    Translation available in German.

Absence from Felicity: The Story of Helen Schucman and Her Scribing of *A Course in Miracles*. Second edition.
ISBN 978-0-933291-08-9 • #B-11 • Paperback • 498 pages • $17.

    Translation available in German.

Overeating: A Dialogue. An Application of the Principles of *A Course in Miracles*. Second edition.
ISBN 978-0-933291-11-9 • #B-12 • Paperback • 70 pages • $5.

***A Course in Miracles* and Christianity: A Dialogue.** Kenneth Wapnick and W. Norris Clarke, S.J.
ISBN 978-0-933291-18-8 • #B-13 • Paperback • 110 pages • $7.

    Translations available in Spanish and German.

The Most Commonly Asked Questions About *A Course in Miracles*. Gloria and Kenneth Wapnick.
ISBN 978-0-933291-21-8 • #B-14 • Paperback • 144 pages • $8.

Translations available in Spanish, German, and Dutch.

The Message of *A Course in Miracles*. **Volume One: All Are Called. Volume Two: Few Choose to Listen.**
Two Volumes: 619 pages.
ISBN 978-0-933291-25-6 • #B-15 • Paperback • $22 (set).

Translations available in Spanish and German.

The Journey Home: "The Obstacles to Peace" in *A Course in Miracles*.
ISBN 978-0-933291-24-9 • #B-16 • Paperback • 510 pages • $16.95.

Ending Our Resistance to Love: The Practice of *A Course in Miracles*.
ISBN 978-1-59142-132-0 • #B-17 • Paperback • 94 pages • $7.

Life, Death, and Love: Shakespeare's Great Tragedies and *A Course in Miracles*. **Four-volume set based on** *King Lear, Hamlet, Macbeth,* **and** *Othello*.
Four Volumes: 383 pages.
ISBN 978-1-59142-142-9 • #B-18 • Paperback • $25 (set).

The Healing Power of Kindness – Volume One: Releasing Judgment.
ISBN 978-1-59142-147-4 • #B-19 • Paperback • 109 pages • $7.

The Healing Power of Kindness – Volume Two: Forgiving Our Limitations.
ISBN 978-1-59142-155-9 • #B-20 • Paperback • 118 pages • $6.

Form versus Content: Sex and Money.
ISBN 978-1-59142-194-8 • #B-21 • Paperback • 116 pages • $7.

Journey through the Workbook of *A Course in Miracles*. Commentary on the 365 Lessons.
Eight Volumes: 1,158 pages.
ISBN 978-1-59142-206-8 • #B-23 • Paperback • $60 (set).

"What It Says": From the Preface of *A Course in Miracles*.
ISBN 978-1-59142-208-2 • #B-25 • Paperback • 78 pages • $8.

The Arch of Forgiveness.
ISBN 978-1-59142-210-5 • #B-27 • Paperback • 103 pages • $7.

Ordering Information

For orders *in the continental U.S. only*, please add $6.00 for the first item, and $1.00 for each additional item, for shipping and handling. The shipping charge for *Journey through the Workbook of A COURSE IN MIRACLES* is $10.00; add $1.00 for each additional item.

For orders to *all other countries* (SURFACE MAIL), and to *Alaska, Hawaii*, and *Puerto Rico* (FIRST CLASS MAIL), please add $6.00 for the first item and $2.00 for each additional item. The shipping charge for *Journey through the Workbook of A COURSE IN MIRACLES* is $10.00; add $2.00 for each additional item.

California State residents please add local sales tax.

VISA, MasterCard, Discover, American Express accepted.

Order from:

Foundation for A COURSE IN MIRACLES
Dept. B
41397 Buecking Drive
Temecula, CA 92590
(951) 296-6261 • FAX (951) 296-5455

Visit our Web site at *www.facim.org*

* * * * *

To order additional copies of this book, send a check or money order (in US funds only) for $6.00 plus shipping to the above address; please see shipping charges above.

A Course in Miracles and other scribed material
may be ordered from:

Foundation for Inner Peace
P.O. Box 598
Mill Valley, CA 94942
(415) 388-2060

A Course in Miracles, Second Edition, Complete:
Hardcover - 6" x 9": $35
Softcover - 6" x 9": $30
Paperback - 5" x 8": $20

Psychotherapy: Purpose, Process and Practice: $6
The Song of Prayer: Prayer, Forgiveness, Healing: $6
The Gifts of God: $21
Concordance of *A Course in Miracles*: $49.95